Adult Coloring Book of

FLOWER

INSPIRATIONS

Beautiful Floral Patterns, Botanical Mandalas,
Gemstones, Lovely Words and More!

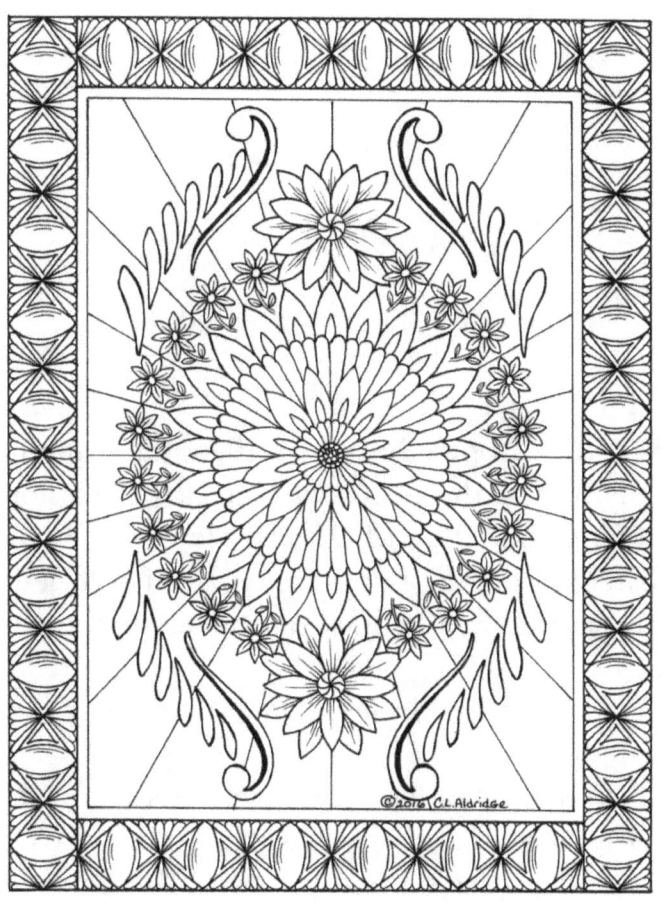

Illustrations by: C. L. Aldridge

ISBN: 10: 1530451167
ISBN-13: 978-1530451166

For all the colorists across the world that
have shared their talent with me and encouraged
me to keep drawing each and every day; and who
gently, and sometimes not so gently requested a second
book, here it is! I hope you enjoy it as much as I enjoyed
drawing it for you. Once again, I Thank You!

And a very special thank you to colorists Virginia Sanders Cole
Sally Thibodeaux, Elizabeth Zack Siegel (front cover l to r),
and Sandi Reutebuch, Tamila Kushnir, Shirley Olsen and Susan
Curry (back cover) for so generously allowing me to use their
colored renderings of my drawings on the cover of this book.

IMPORTANT INFORMATION FOR USING THIS BOOK

- This book contains 24 hand-drawn illustrations, SINGLE SIDED (back is blank).

- Each illustration is printed in TWO SIZES, a full size page and a crafters size (suitable for a 5" x 7" frame, mounting to a greeting card face or scrapbook page, etc). Please note the crafters sizes are also single sided and are printed two on a page.

- The pages are printed on #60 lb bright white paper which performs well for all brands of colored pencils and crayons, without the need of a blotter page.

- To avoid any "Uh Oh's" and the associated disappointment, **Marker and Gel Pen users are STRONGLY ENCOURAGED to USE A BLOTTER SHEET** behind the drawing to avoid any possibility of bleed through to the next page. Several blank blotter and color testing pages are provided at the end of this book.

- Most IMPORTANT of all: Relax, have fun, stand-up and stretch often, and remember that sometimes the most beautiful things come from what we think at first are mistakes, but which turn out to be art's way of working magic!

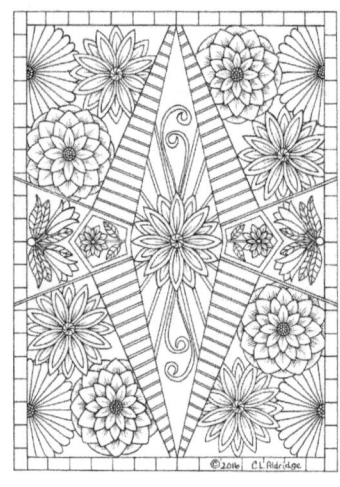
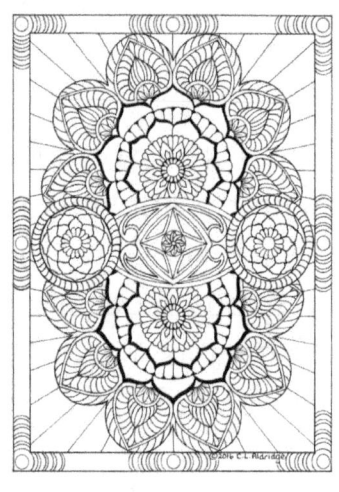
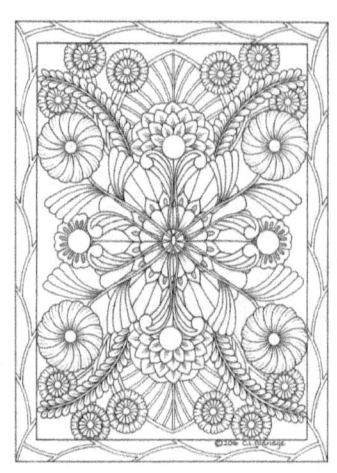
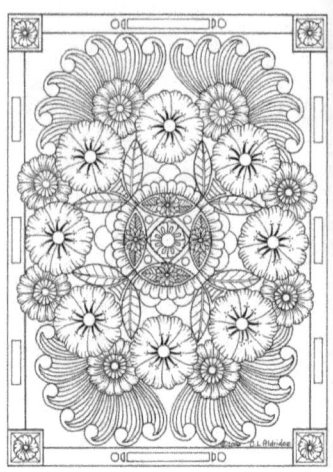
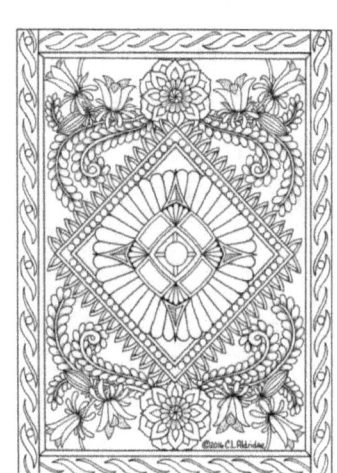
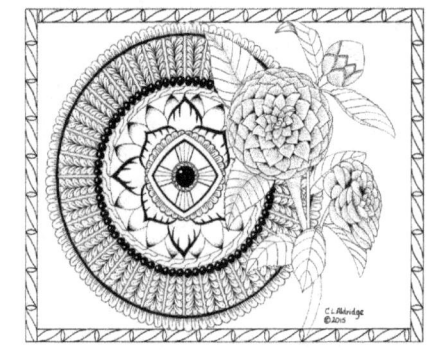
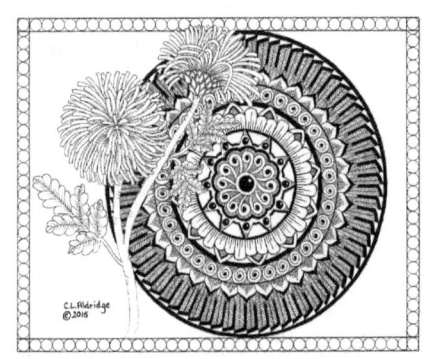
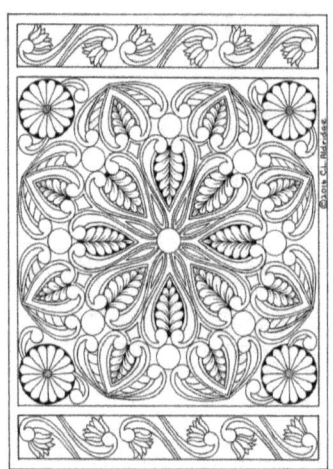
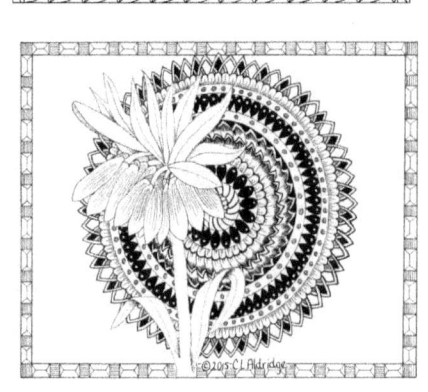
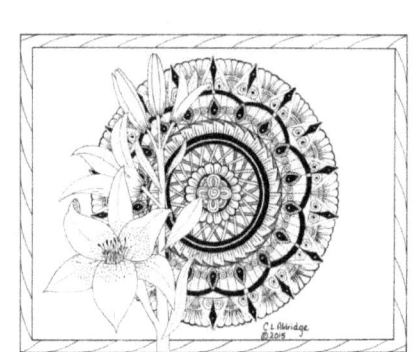
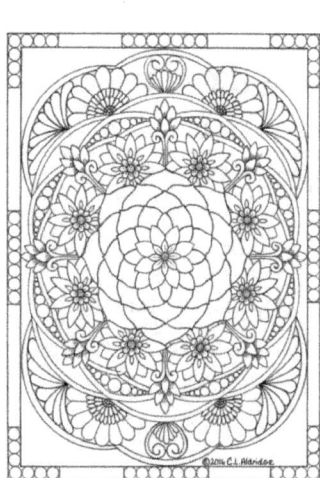
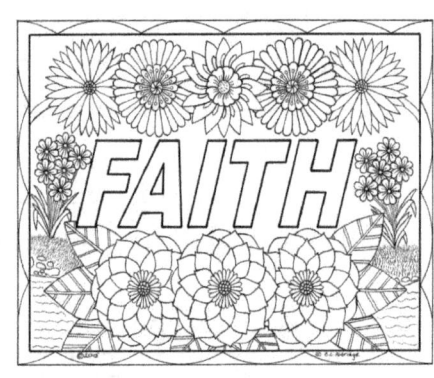
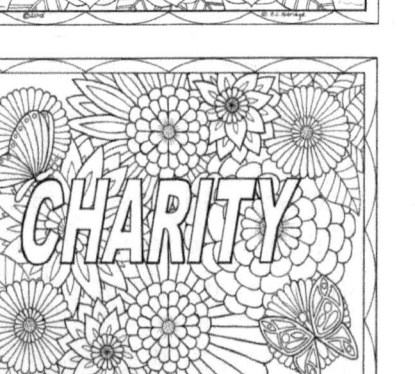
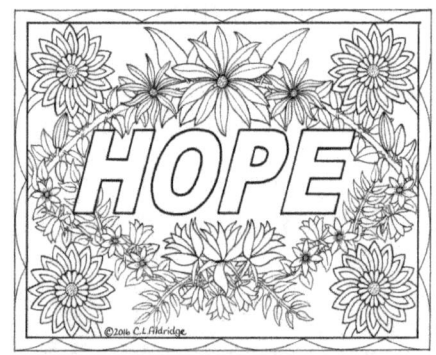
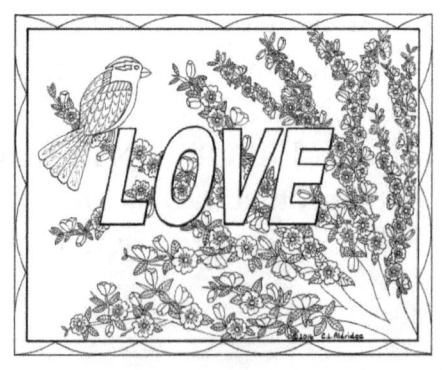

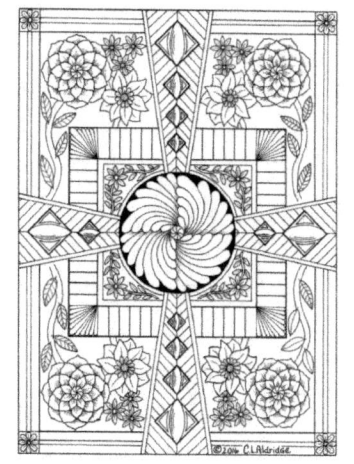
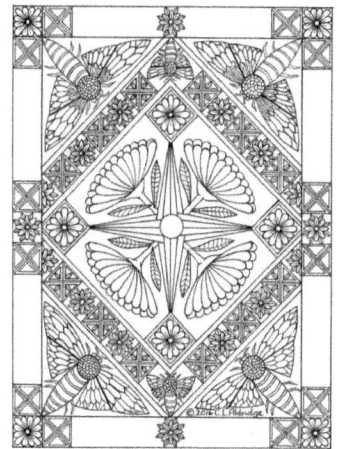
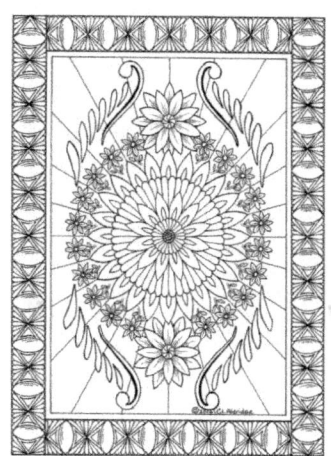
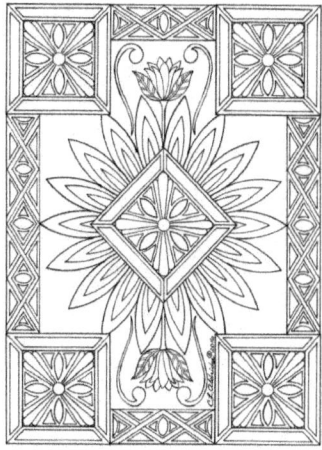

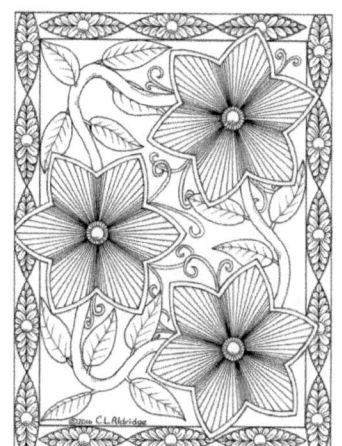
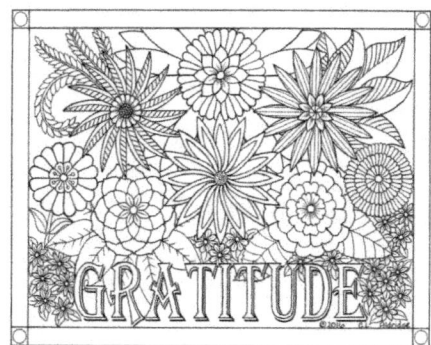
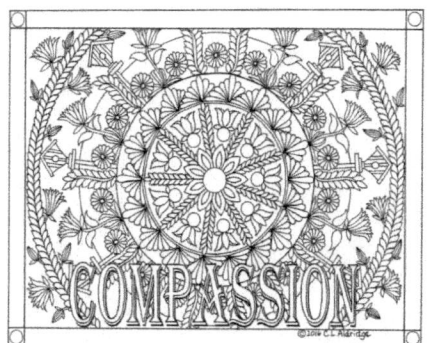
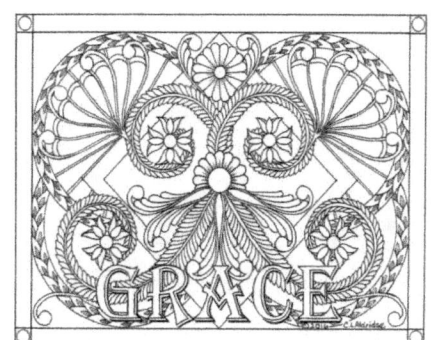
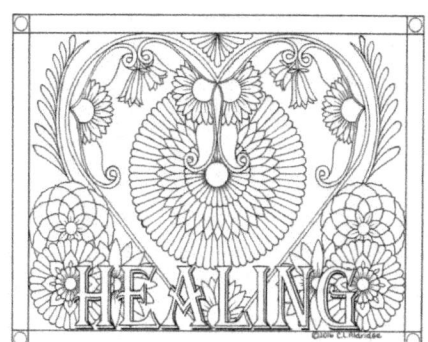

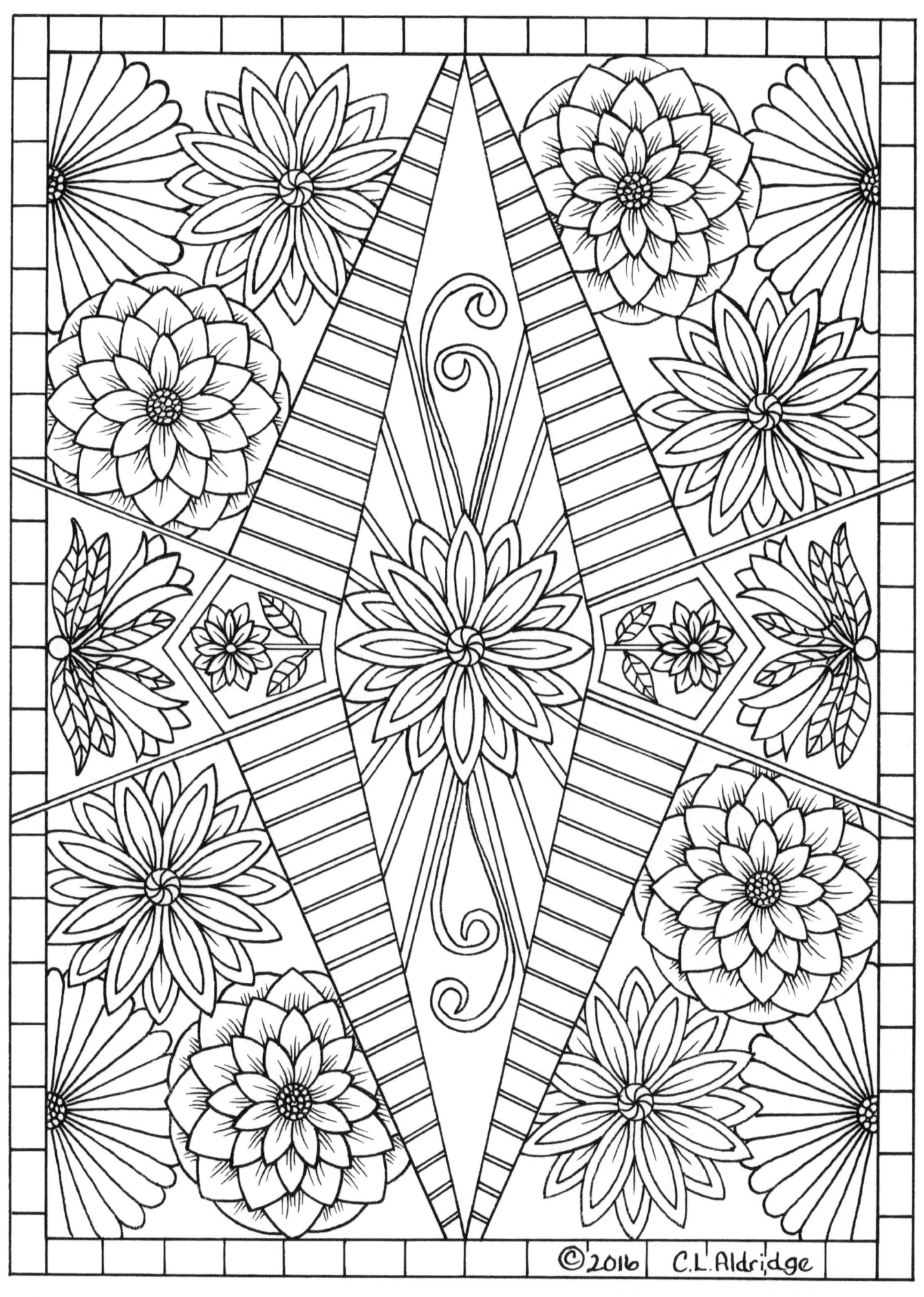

©2016 C.L.Aldridge

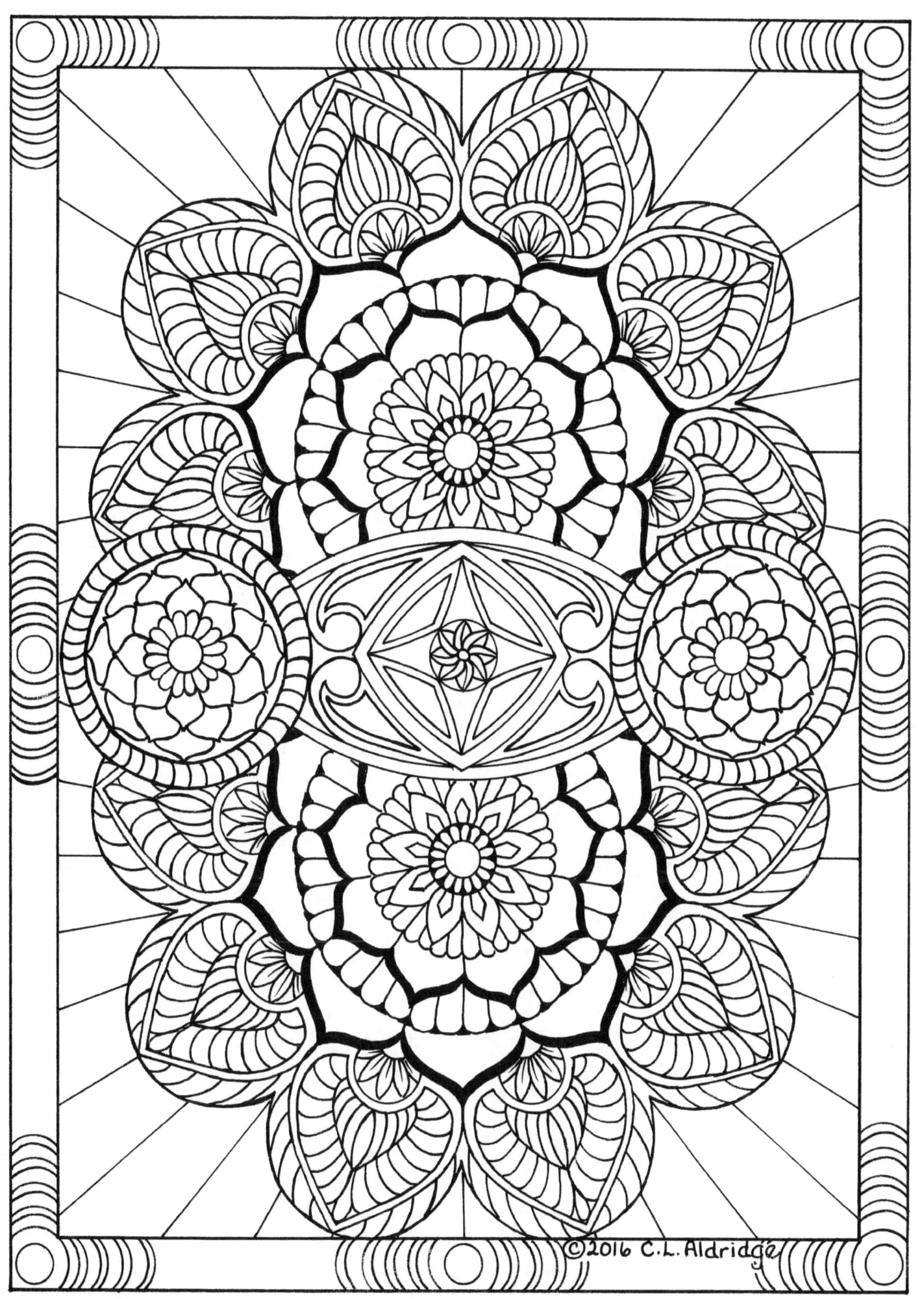
©2016 C.L. Aldridge

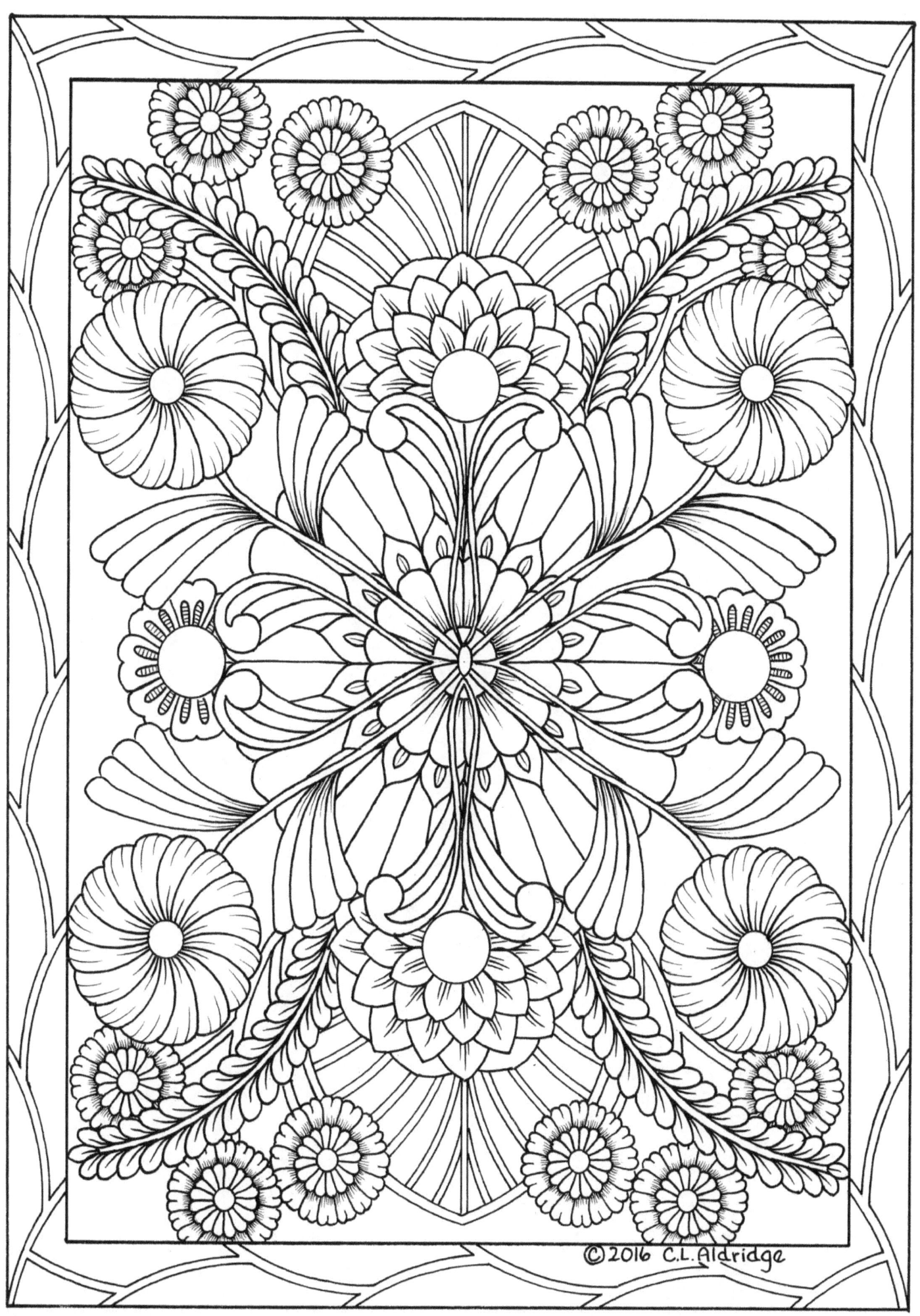

©2016 C.L.Aldridge

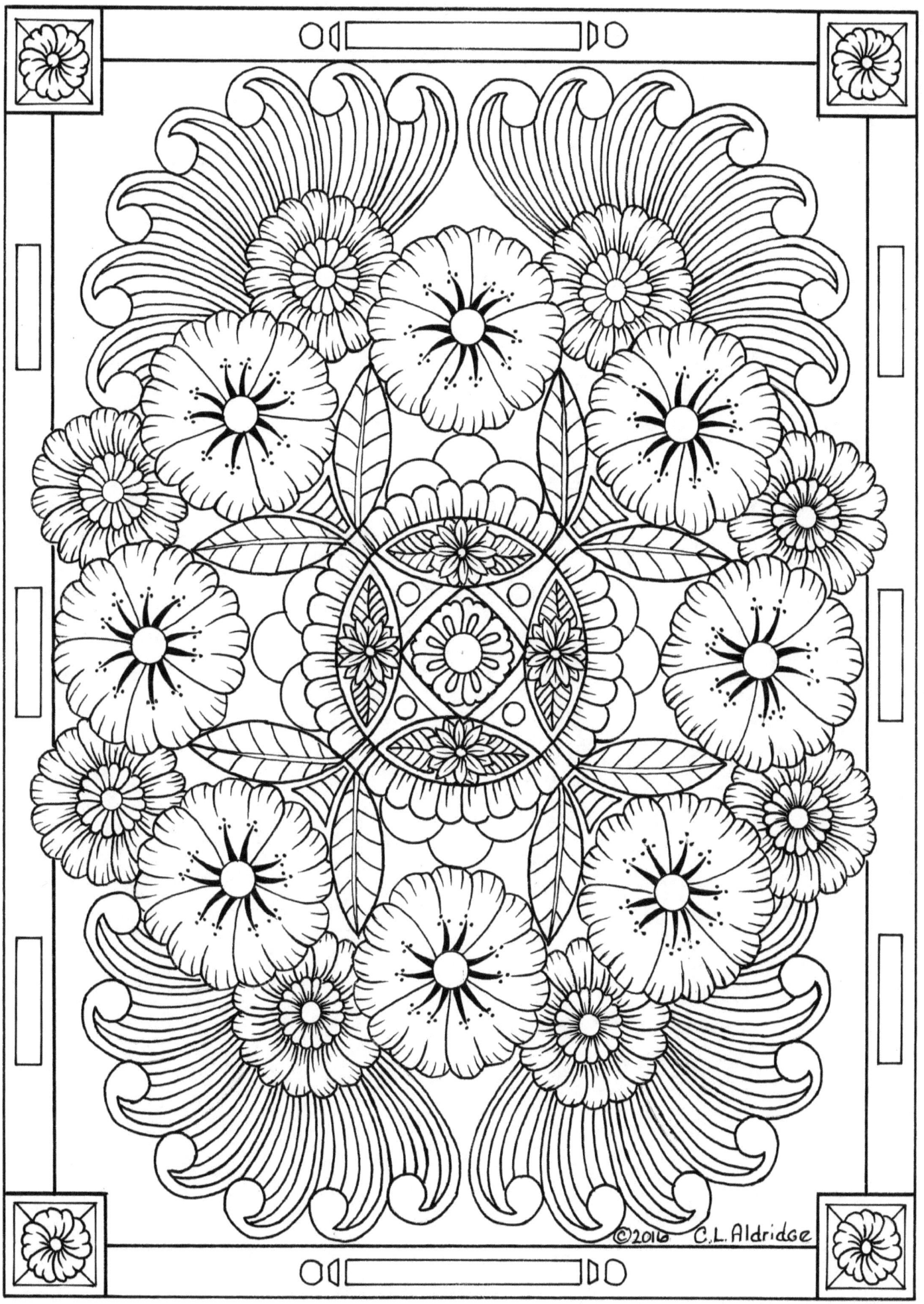

©2016 C.L. Aldridge

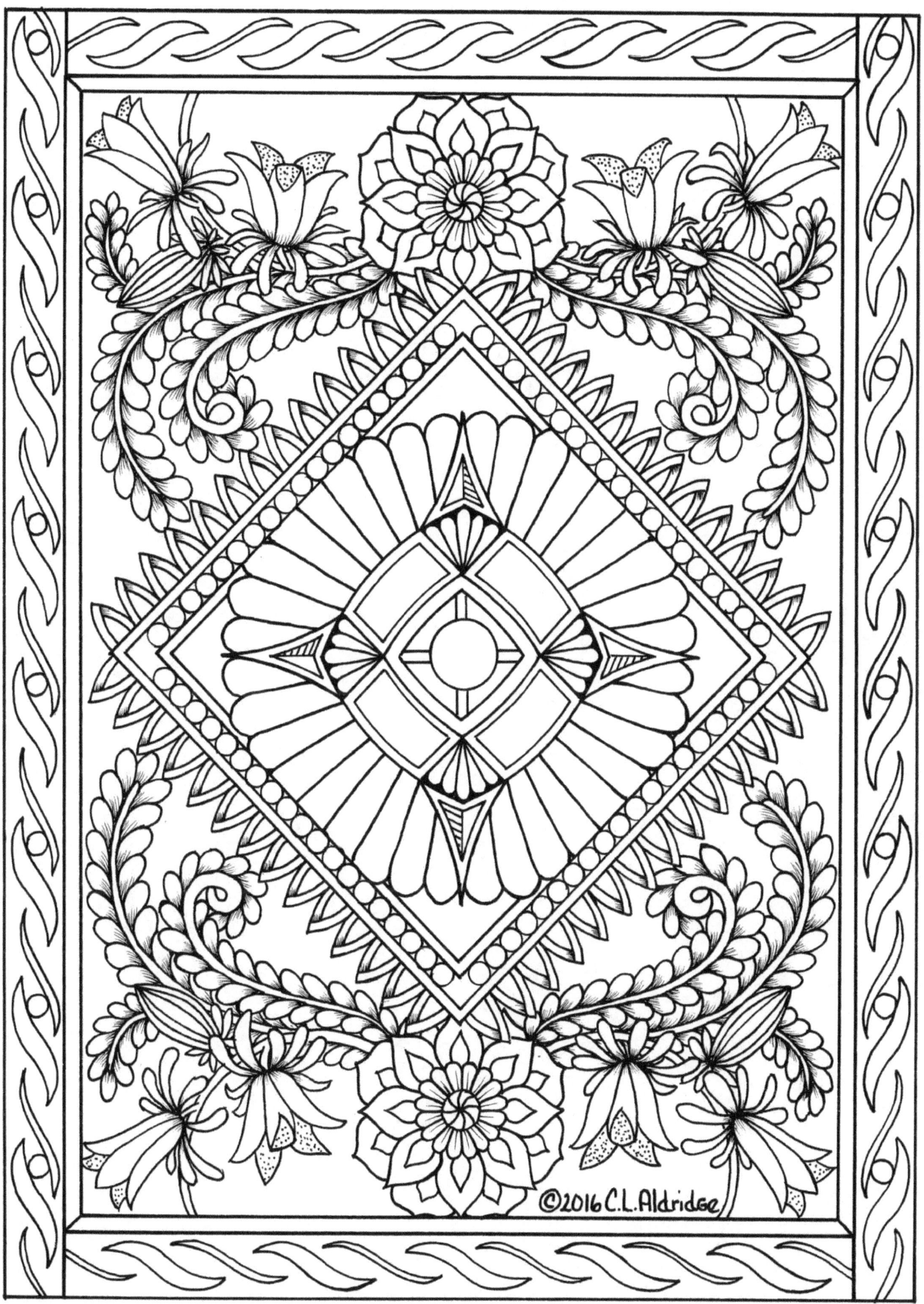

©2016 C.L. Aldridge

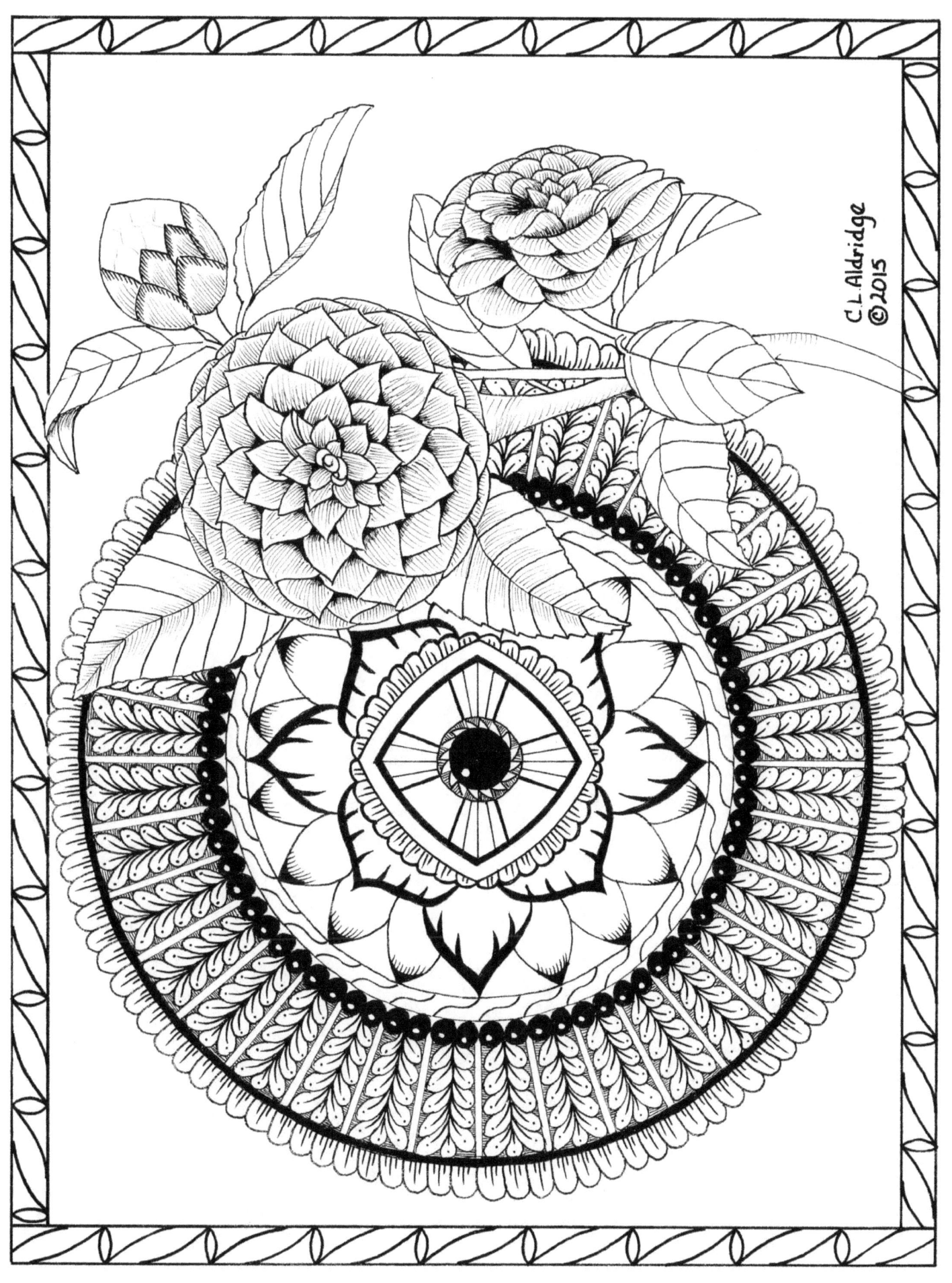

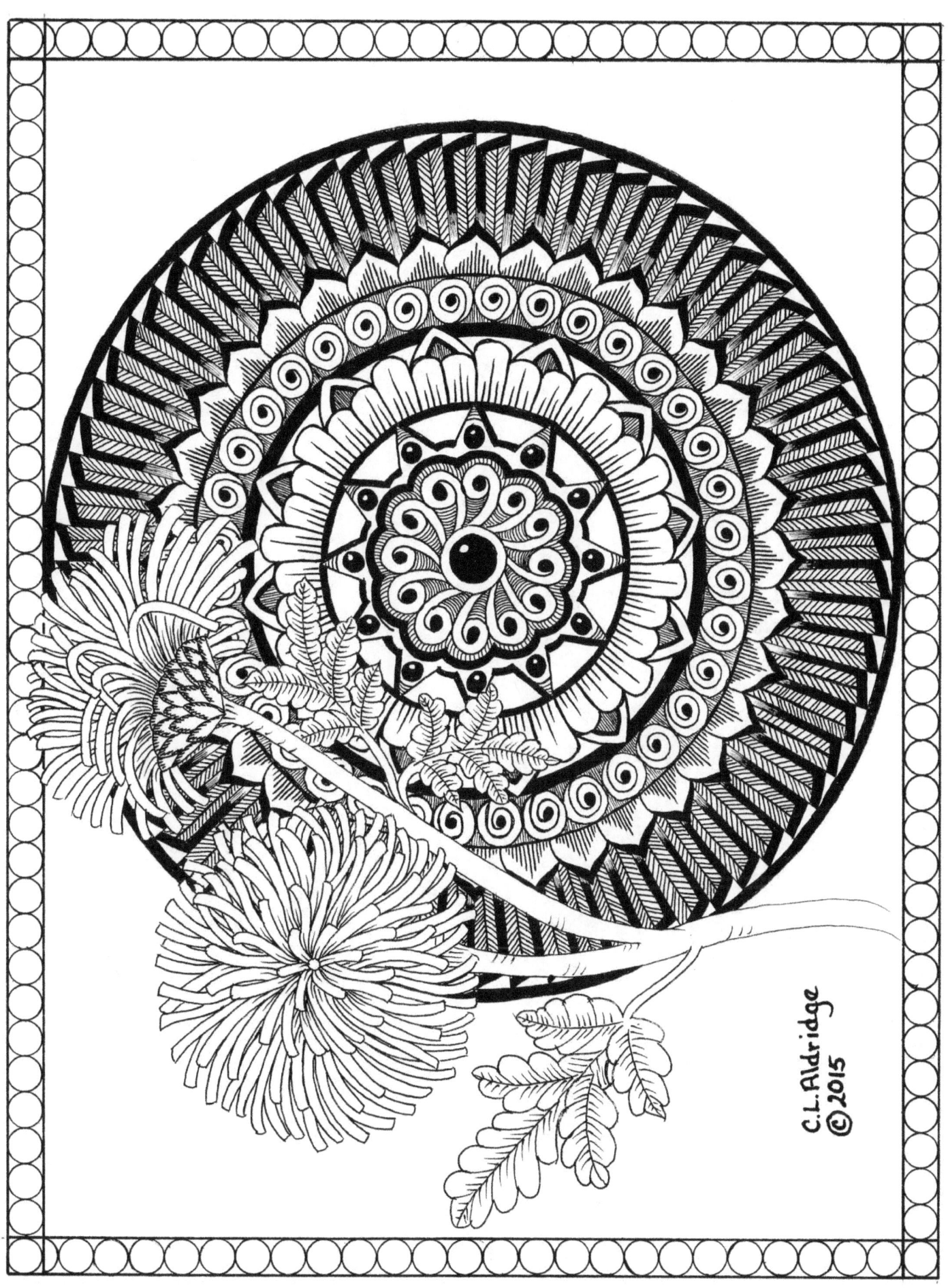

C.L. Aldridge
© 2015

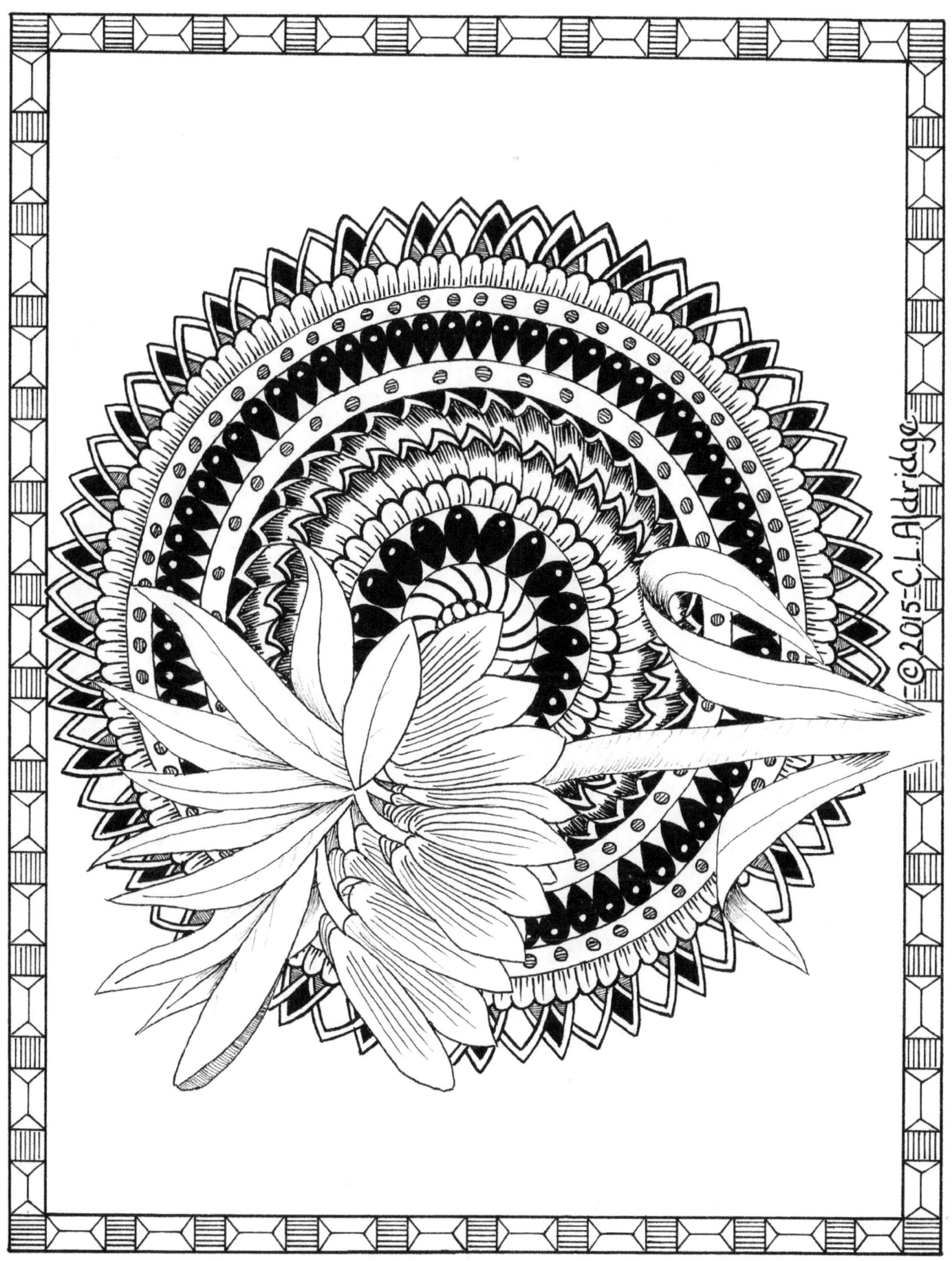

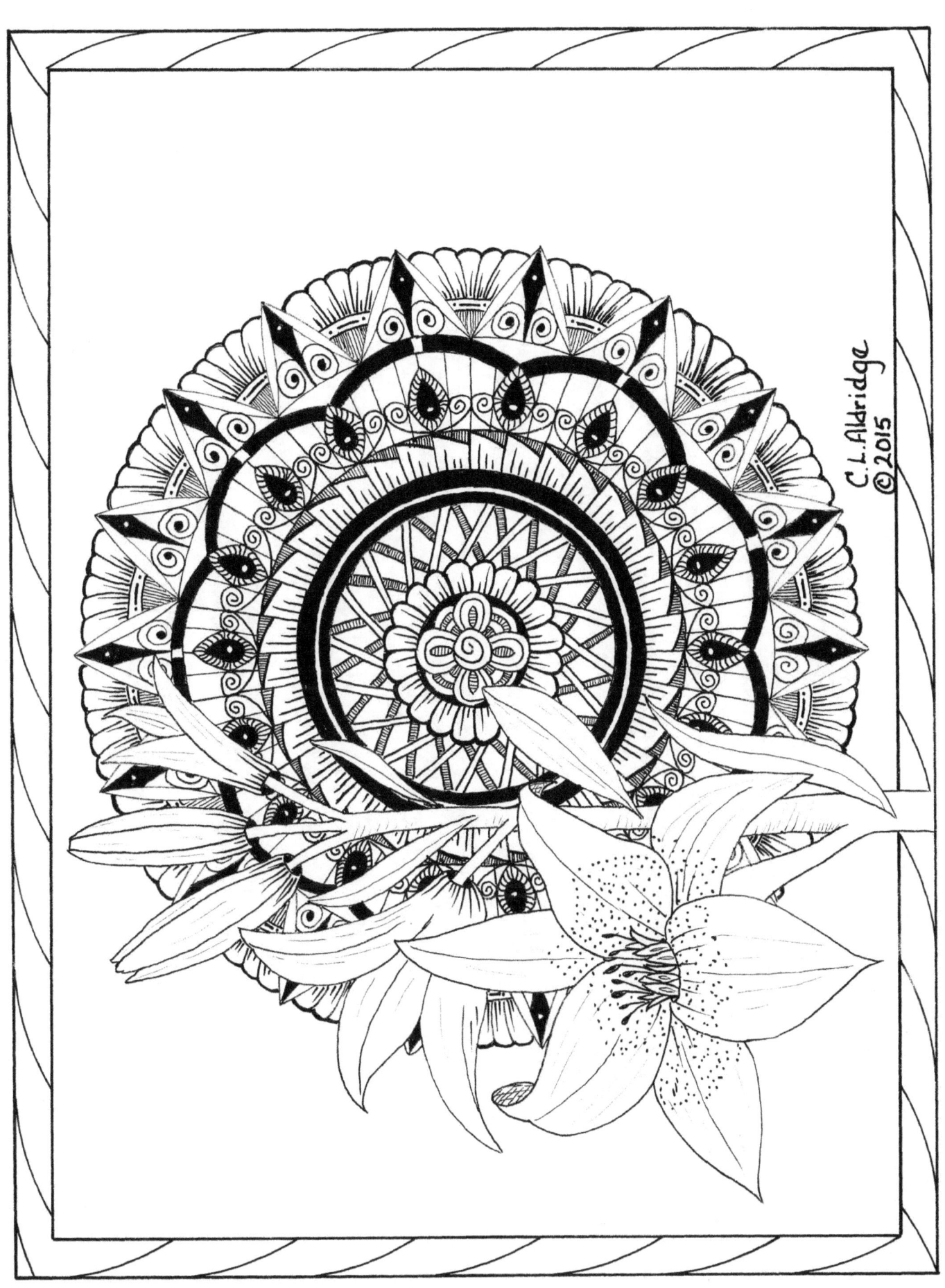

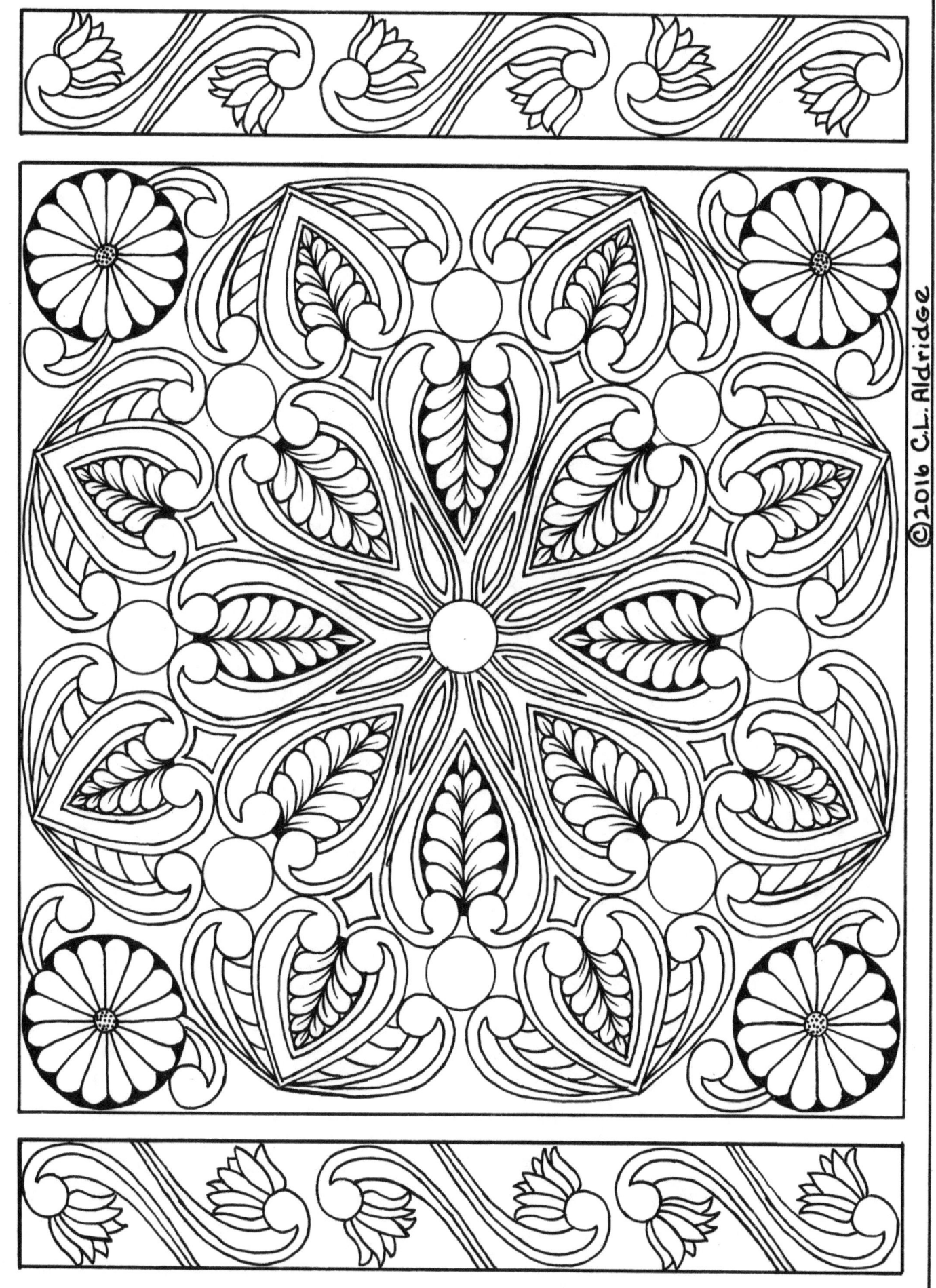

©2016 C.L. Aldridge

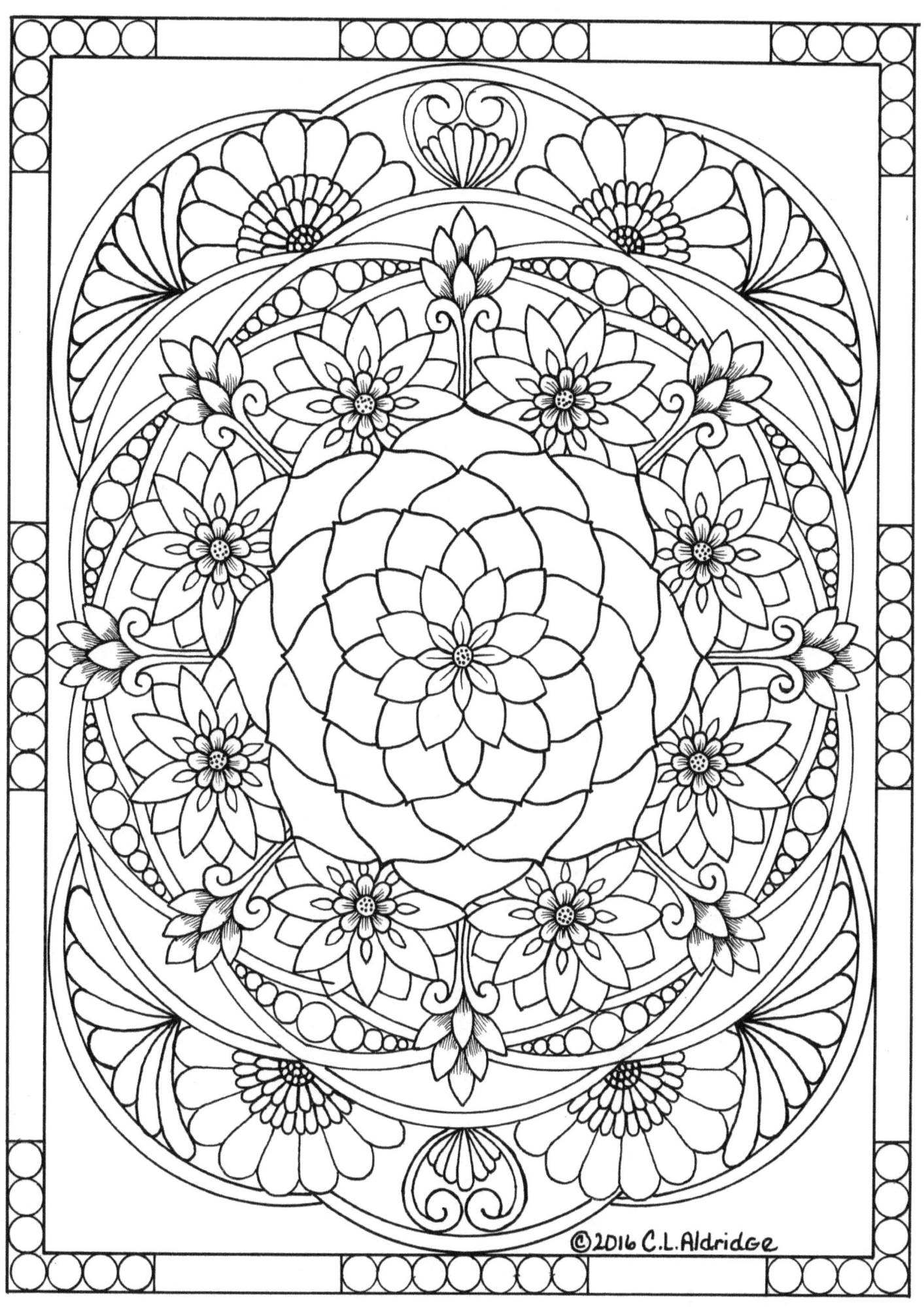

©2016 C.L.Aldridge

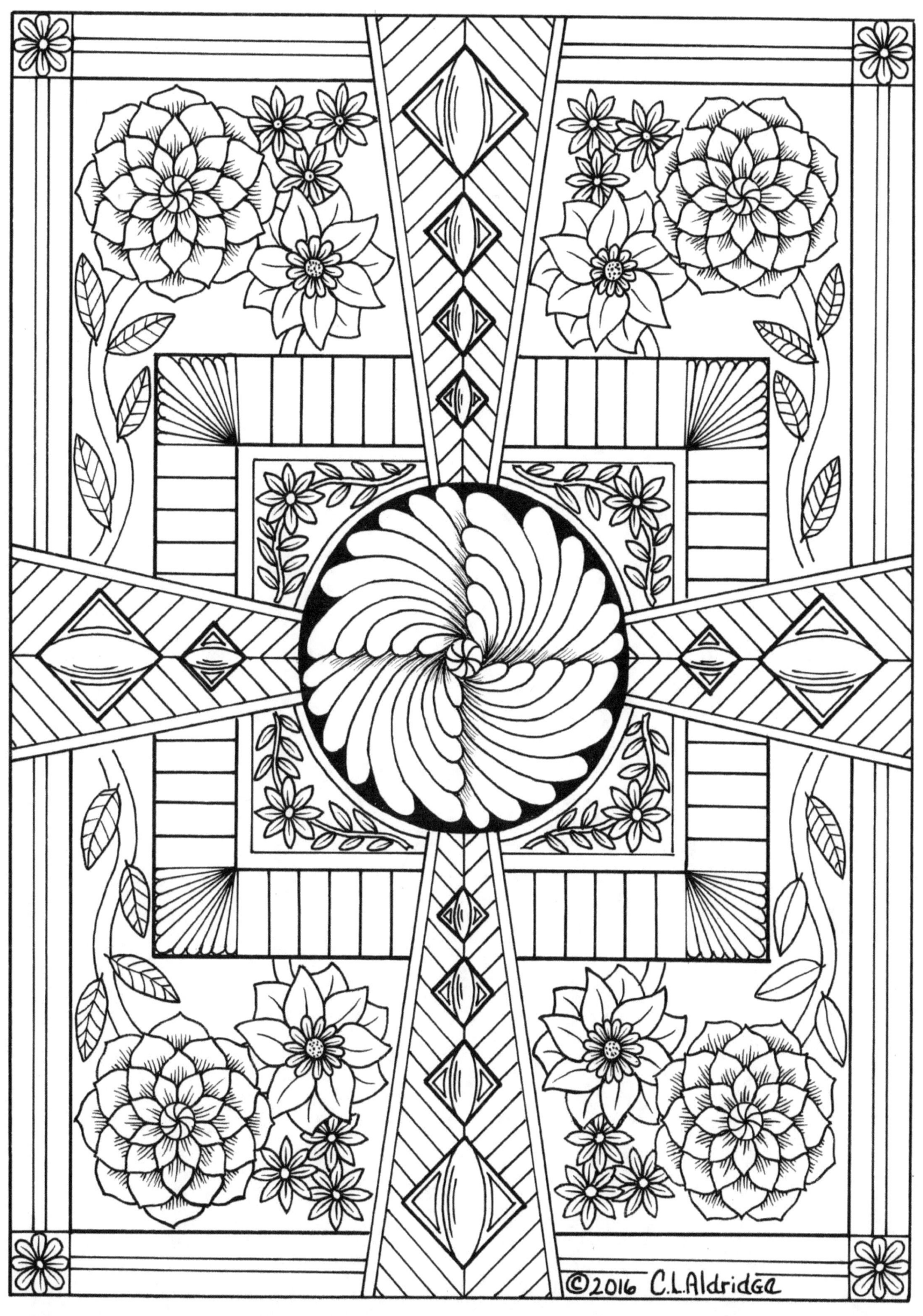

©2016 C.L.Aldridge

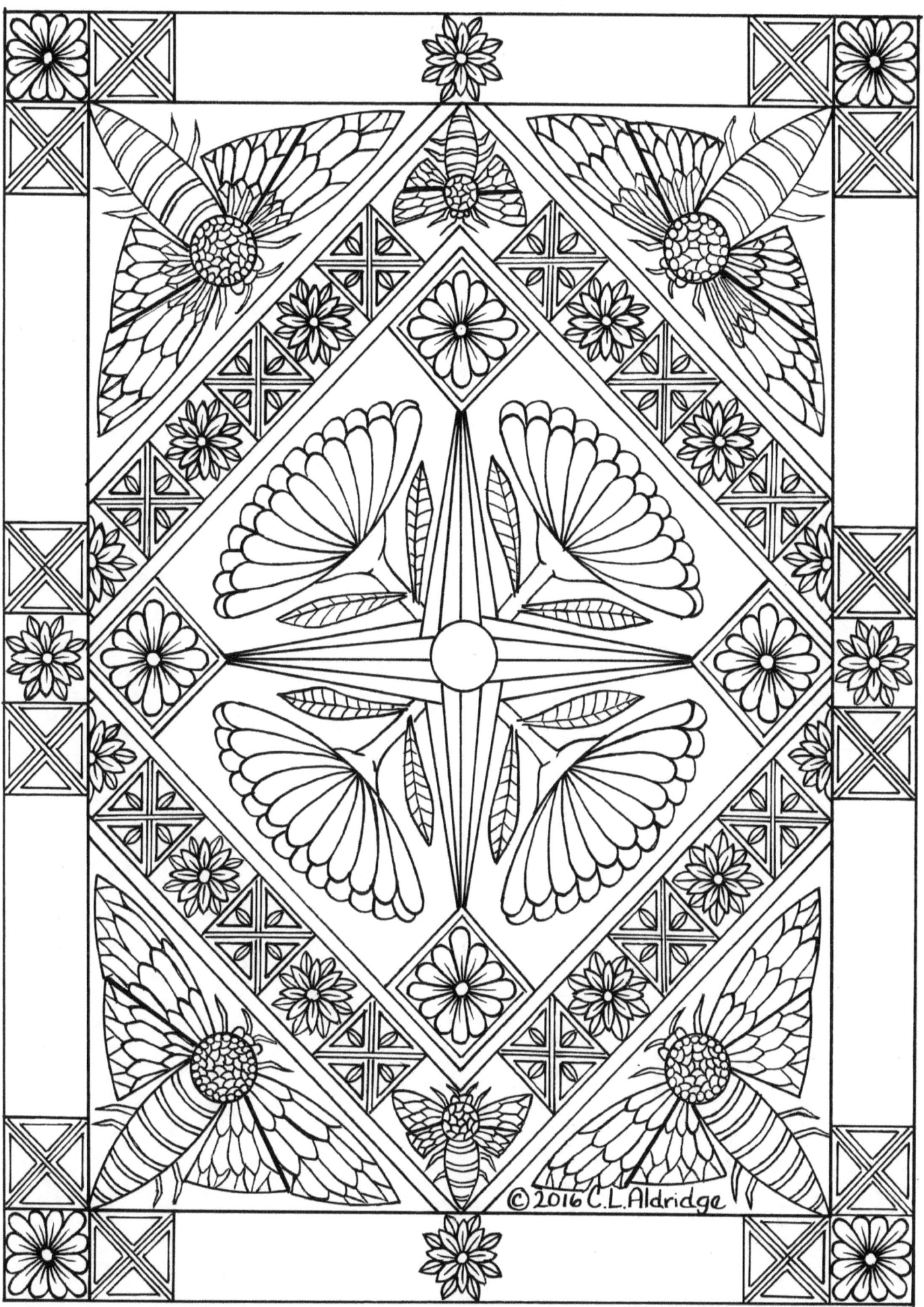

© 2016 C.L.Aldridge

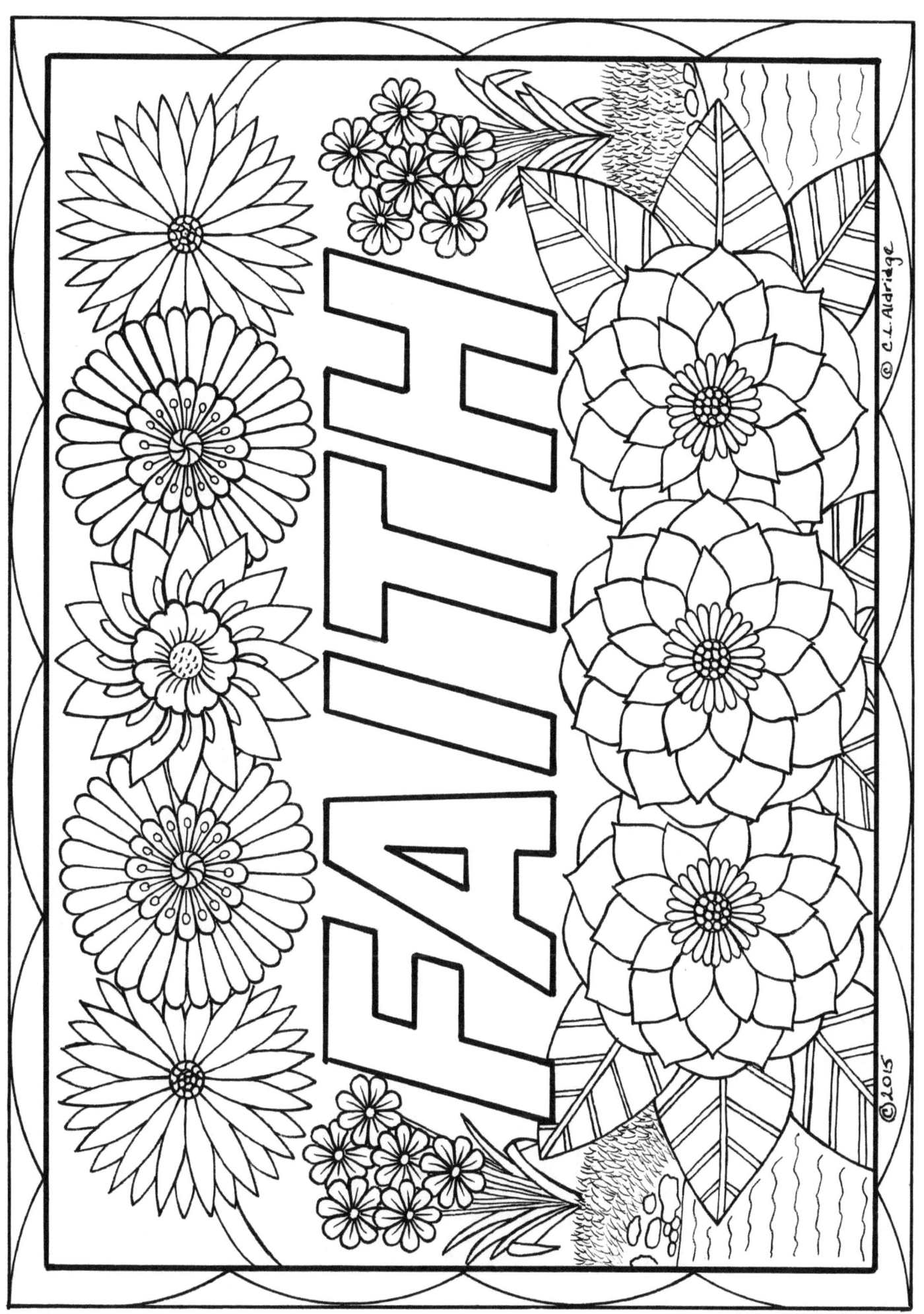

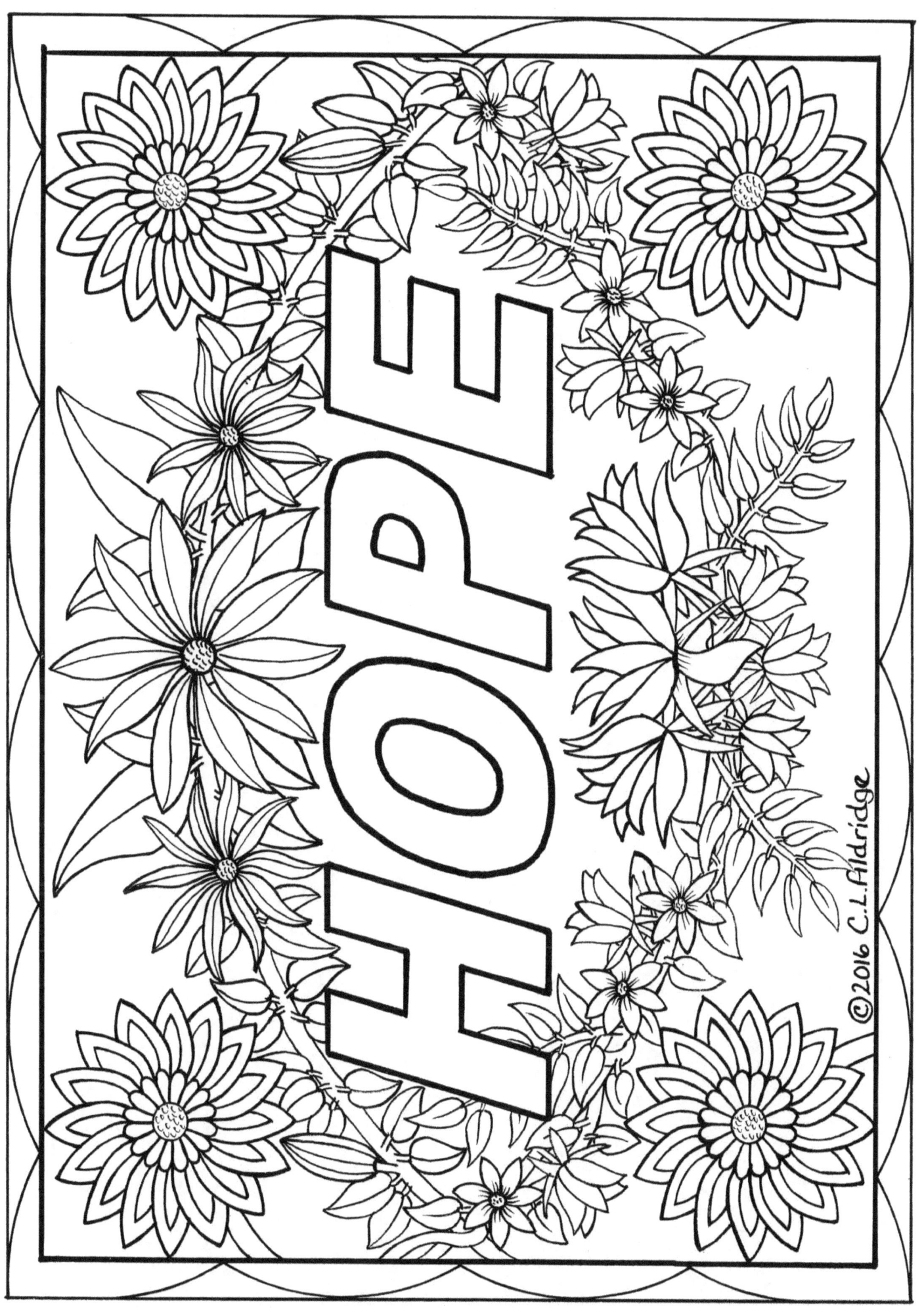

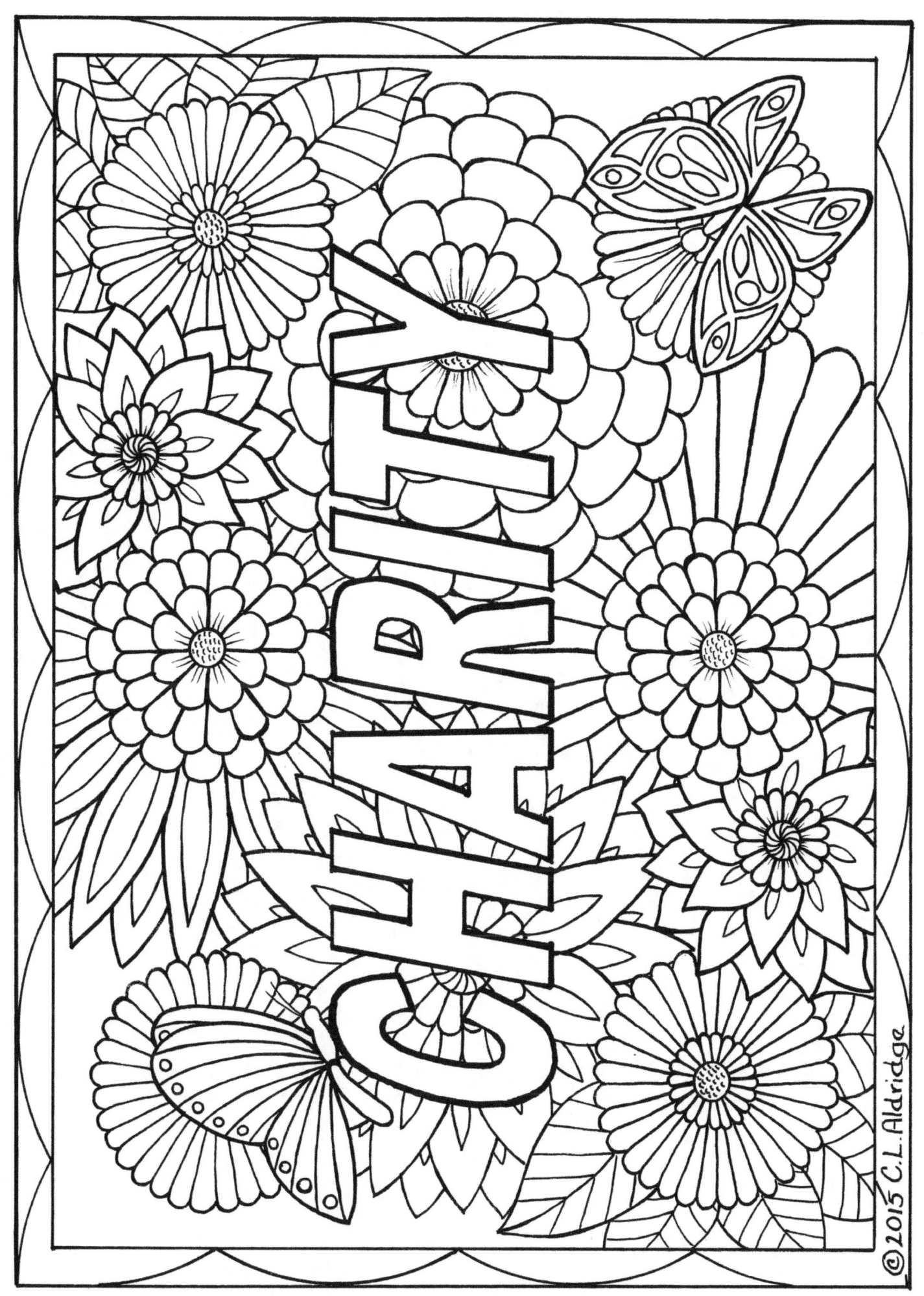

CHARITY

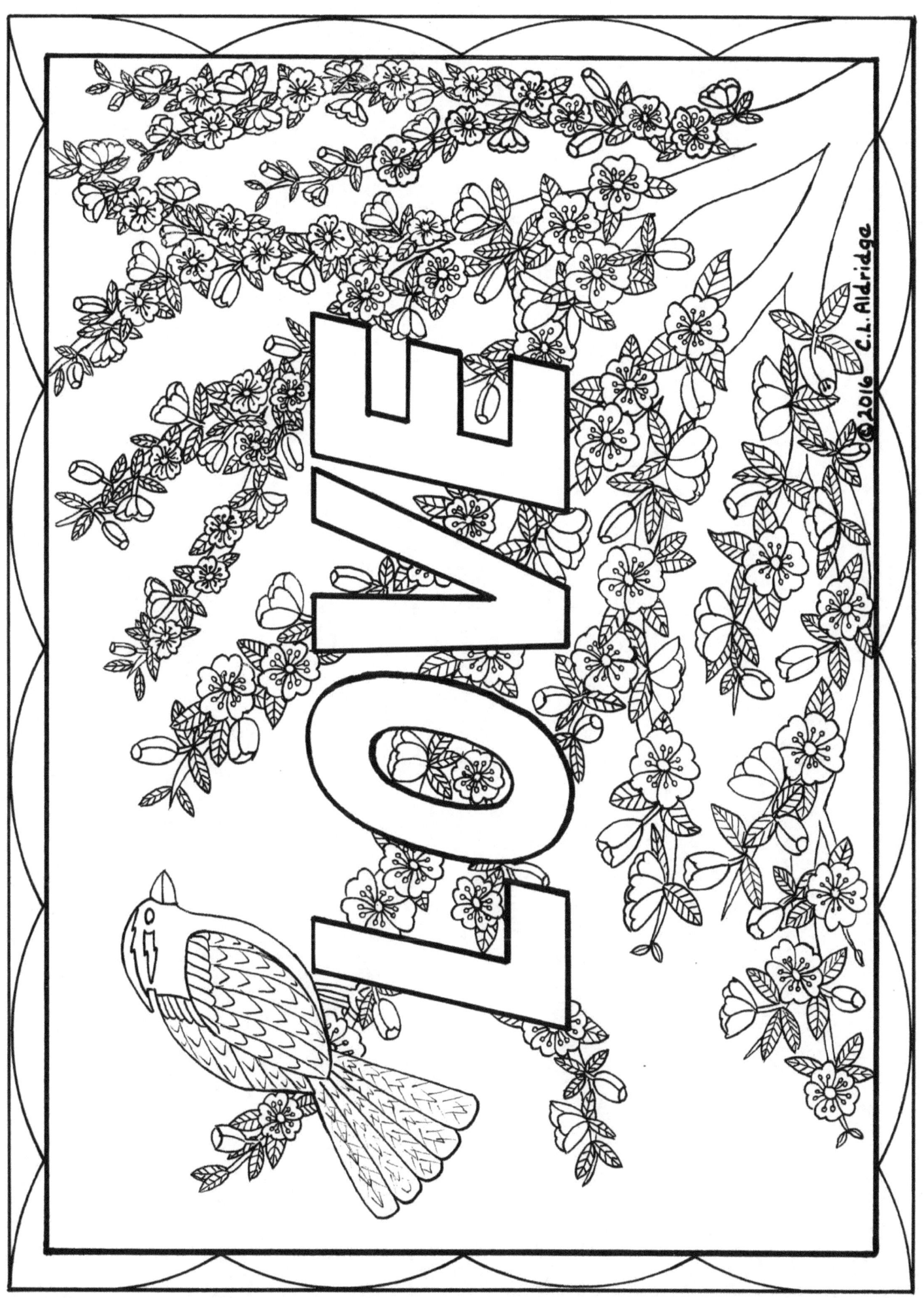

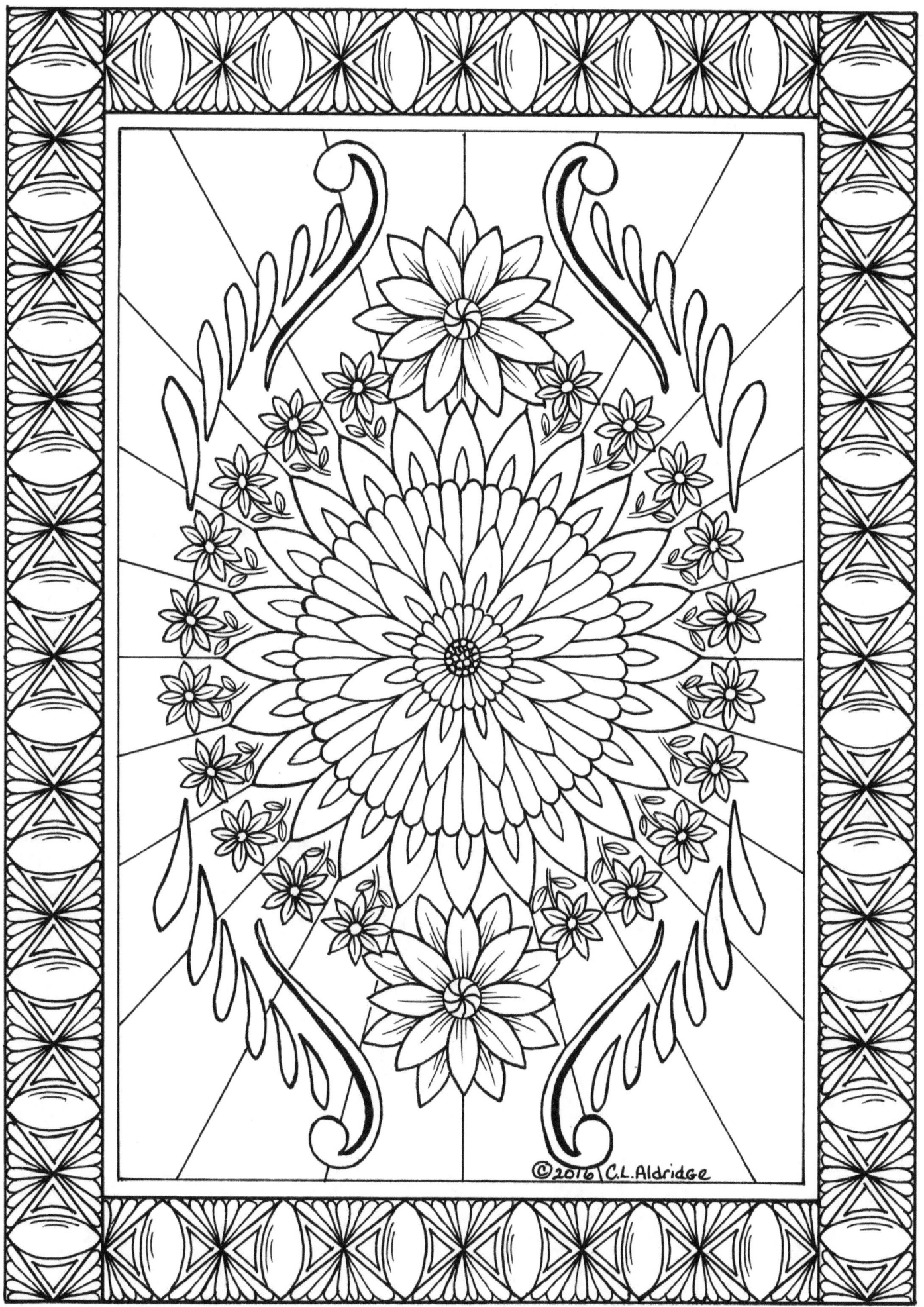
©2016 C.L.Aldridge

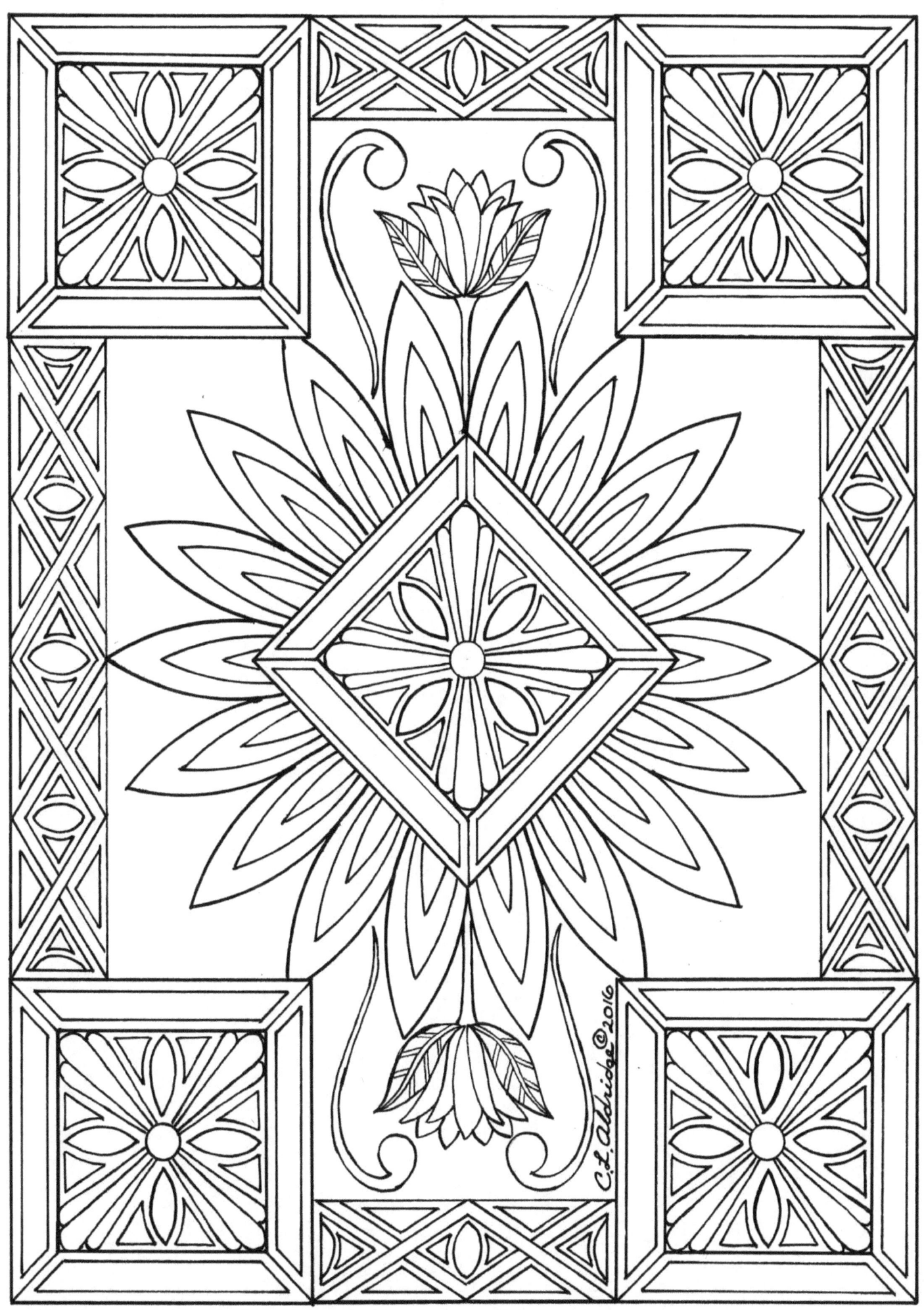

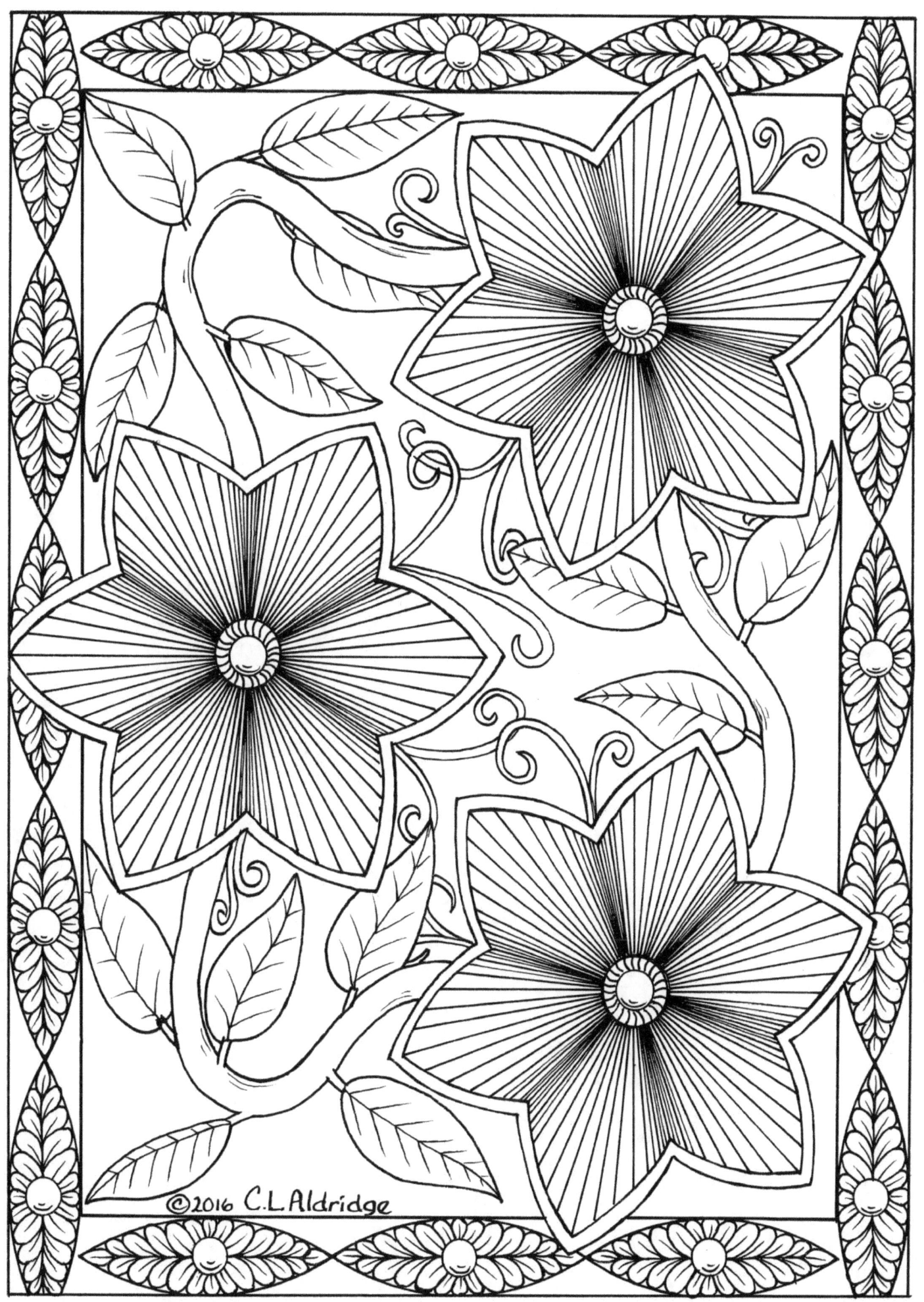

©2016 C.L.Aldridge

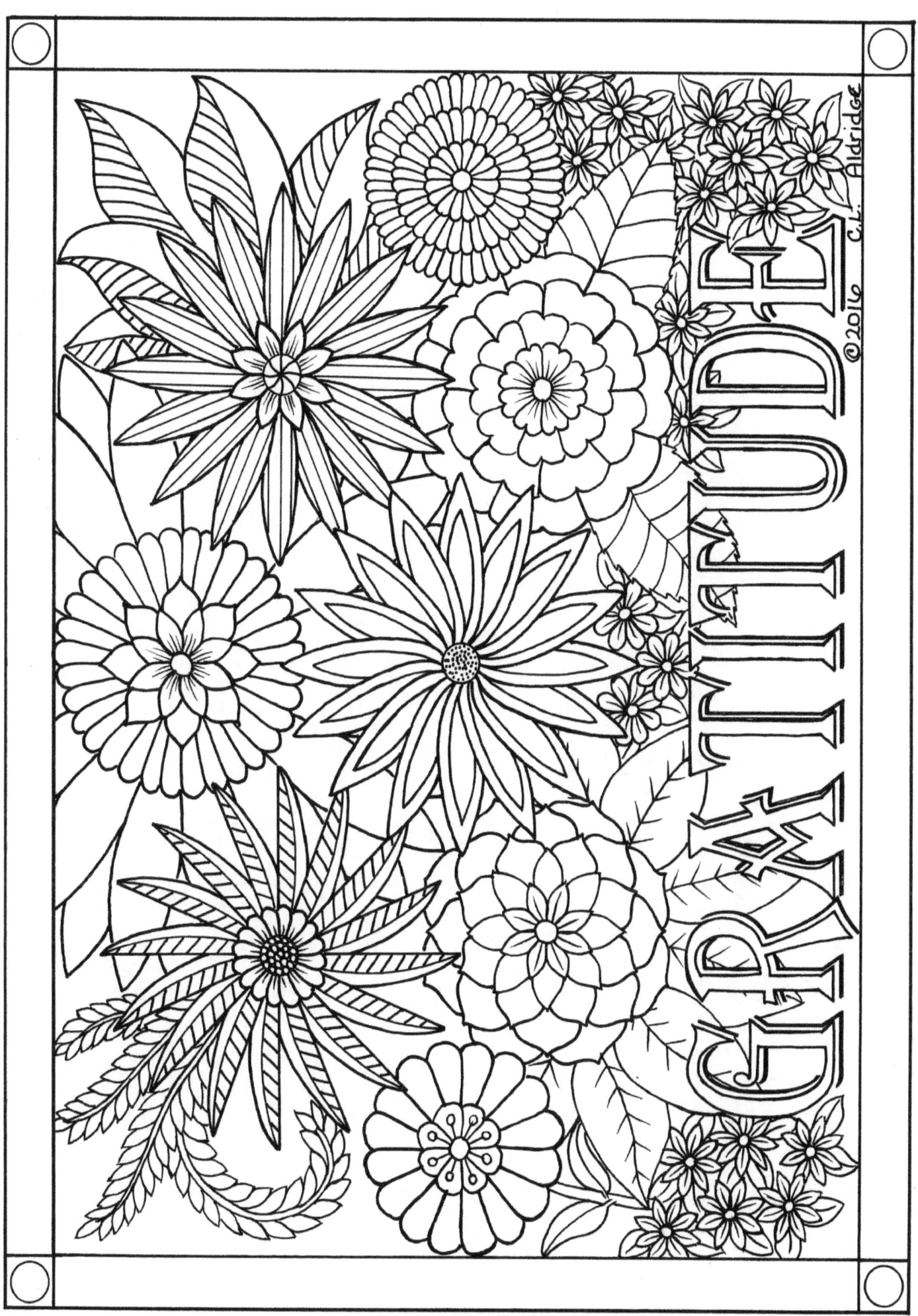

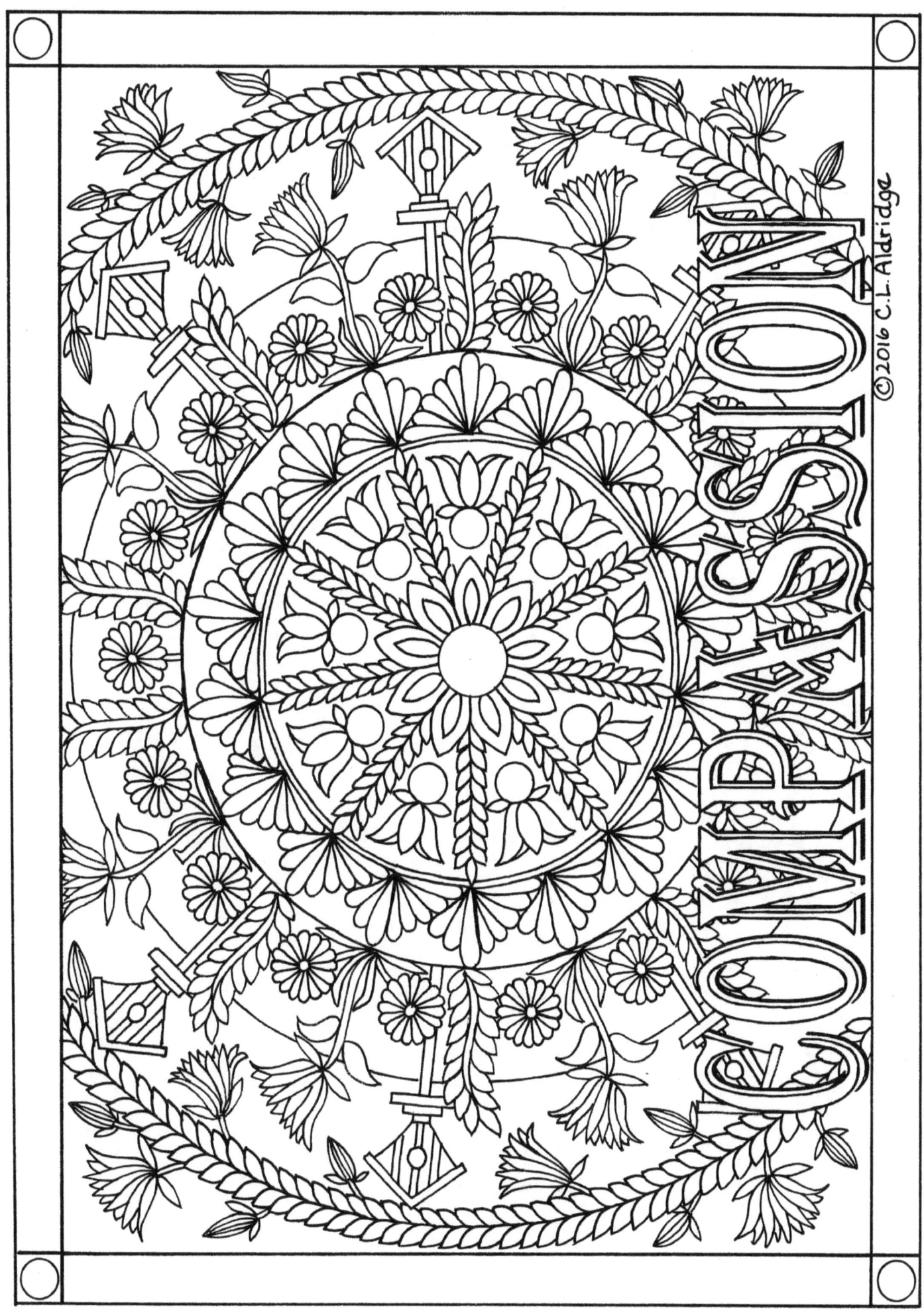

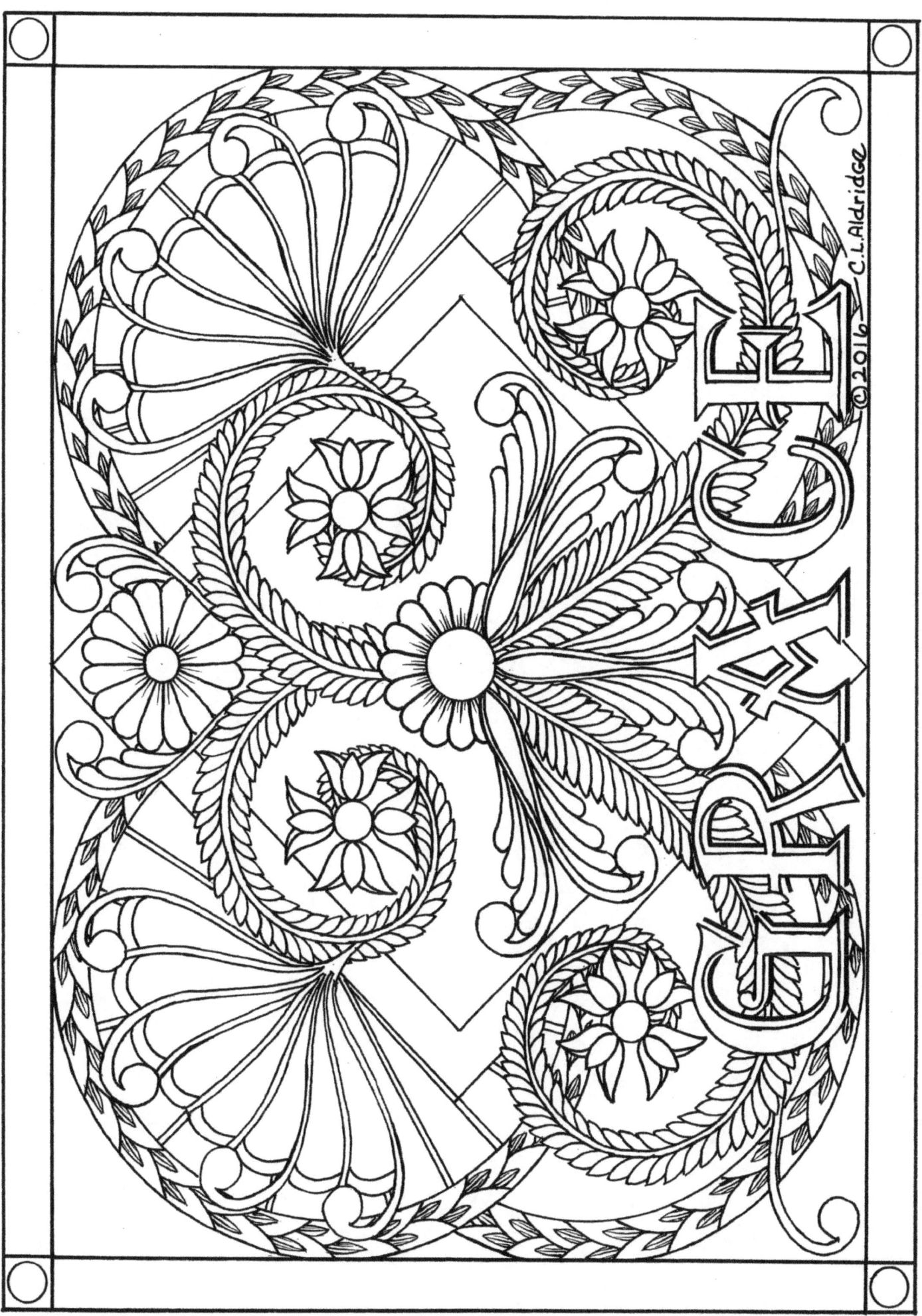

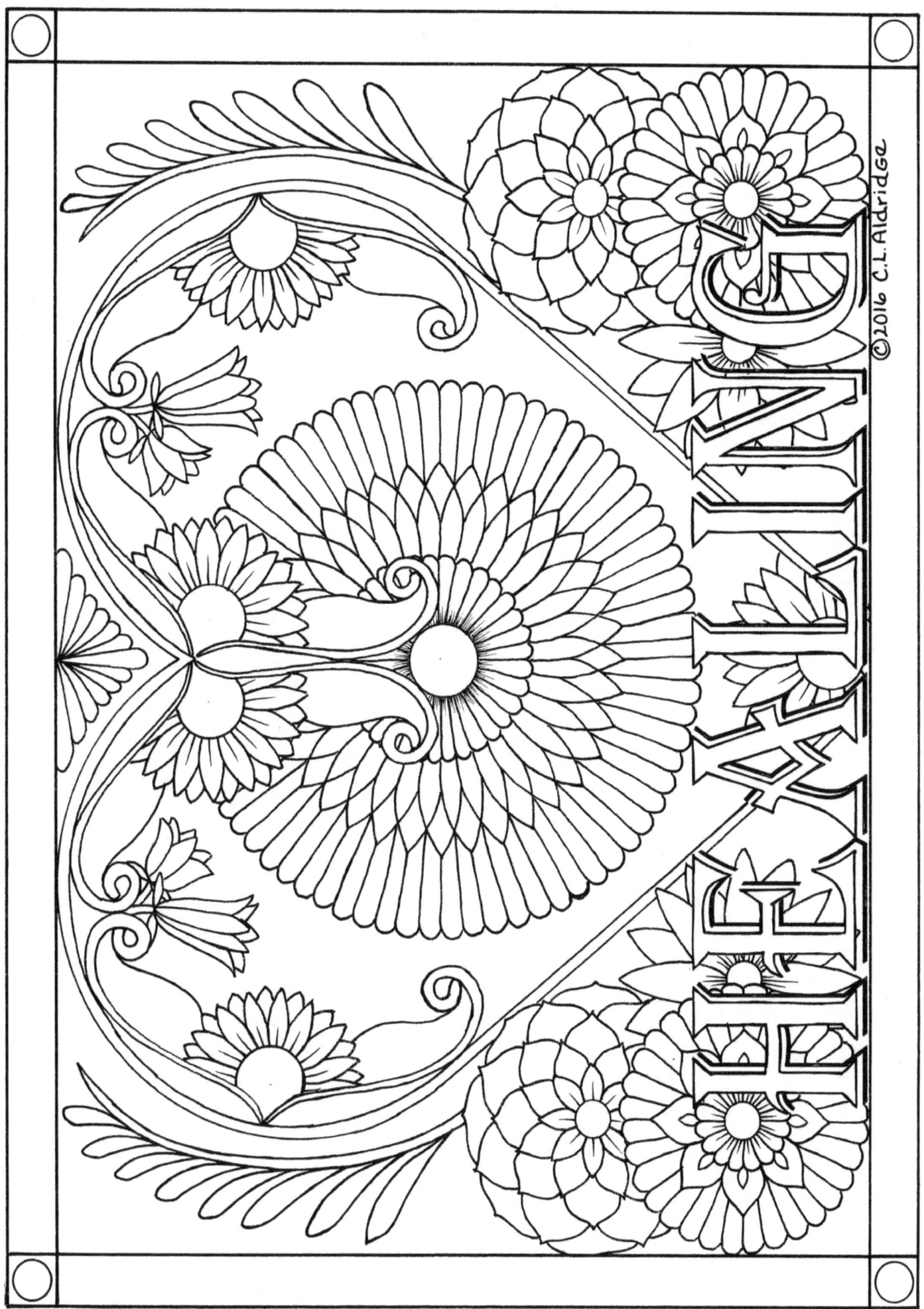

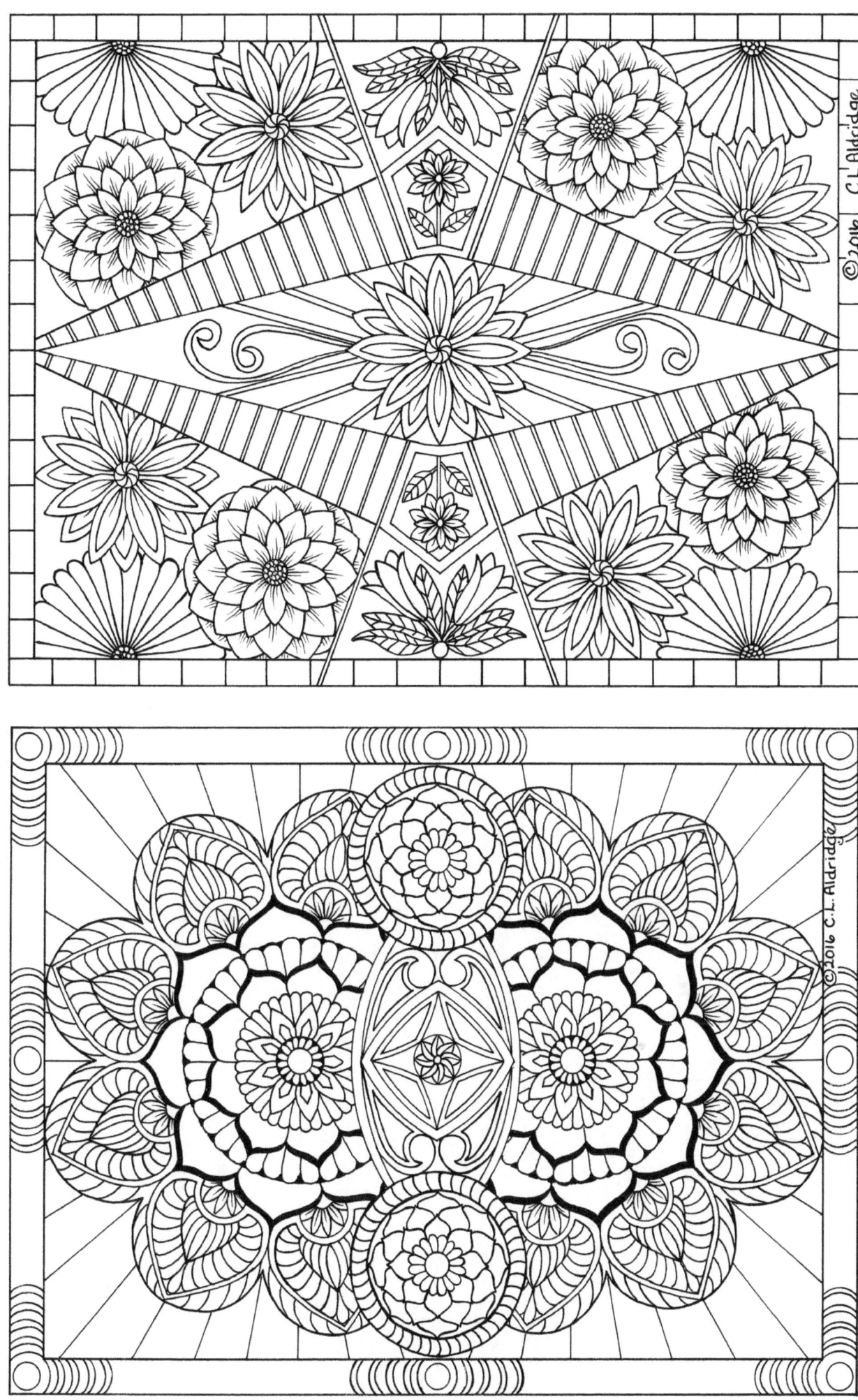

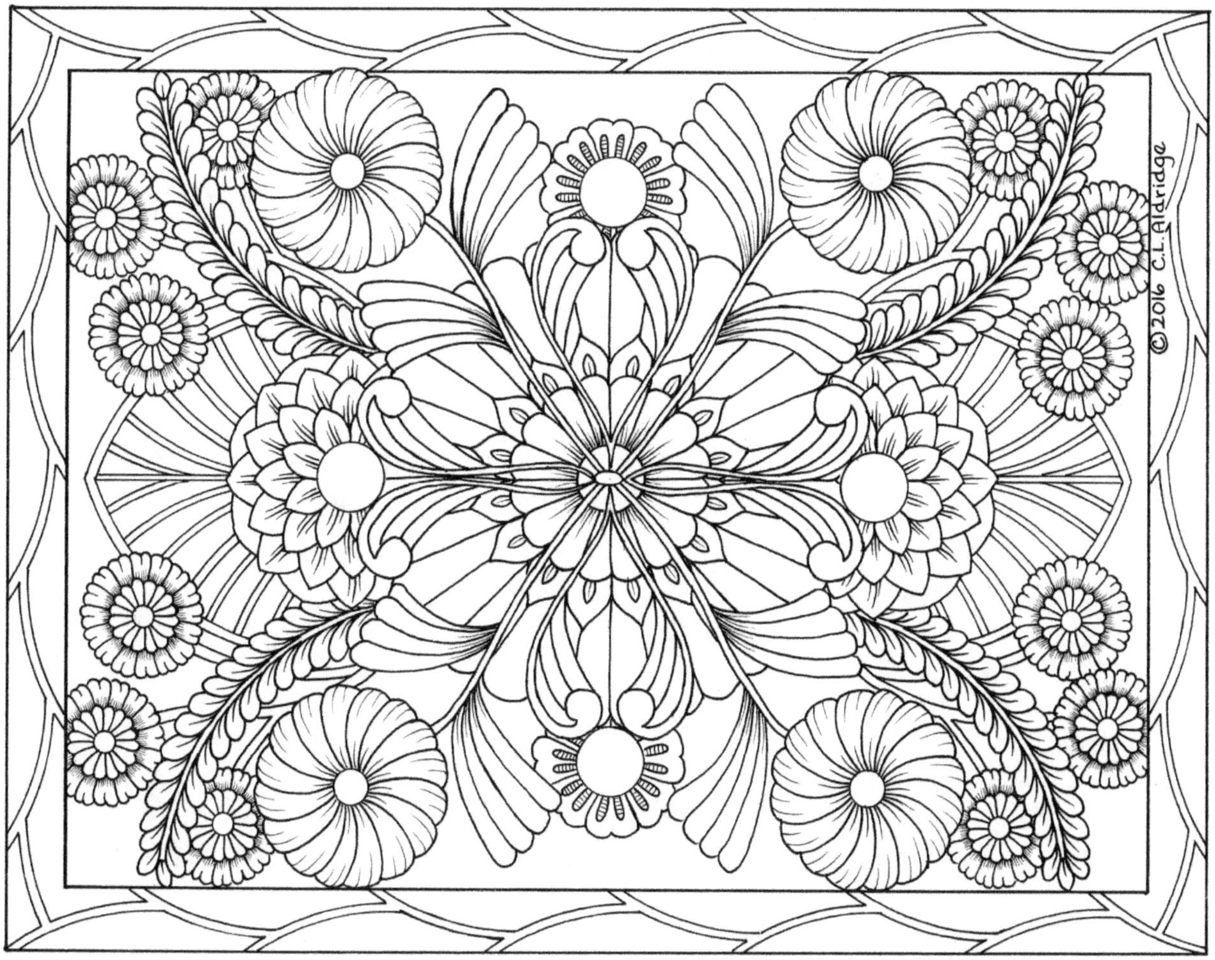
©2016 C.L. Aldridge

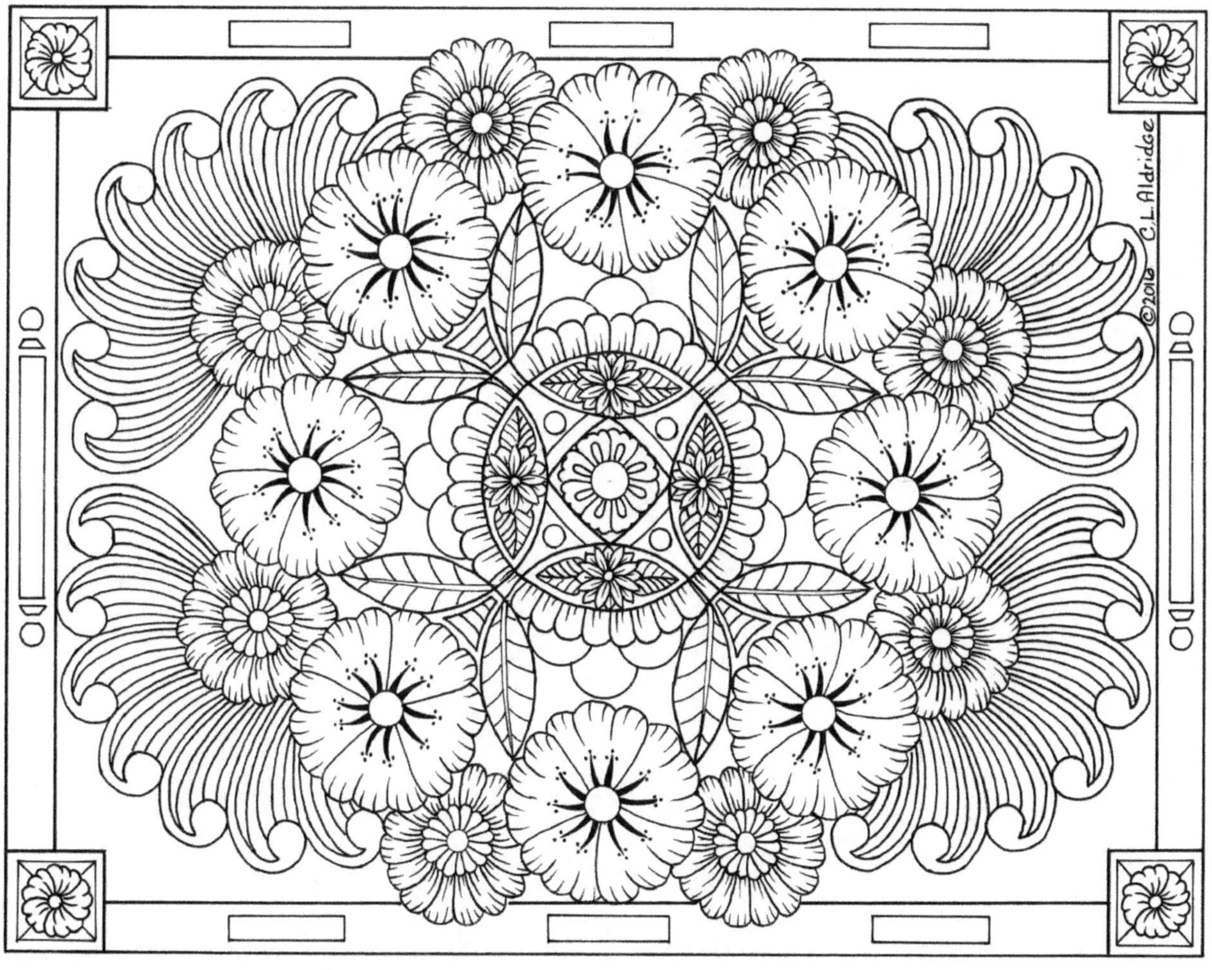
©2016 C.L. Aldridge

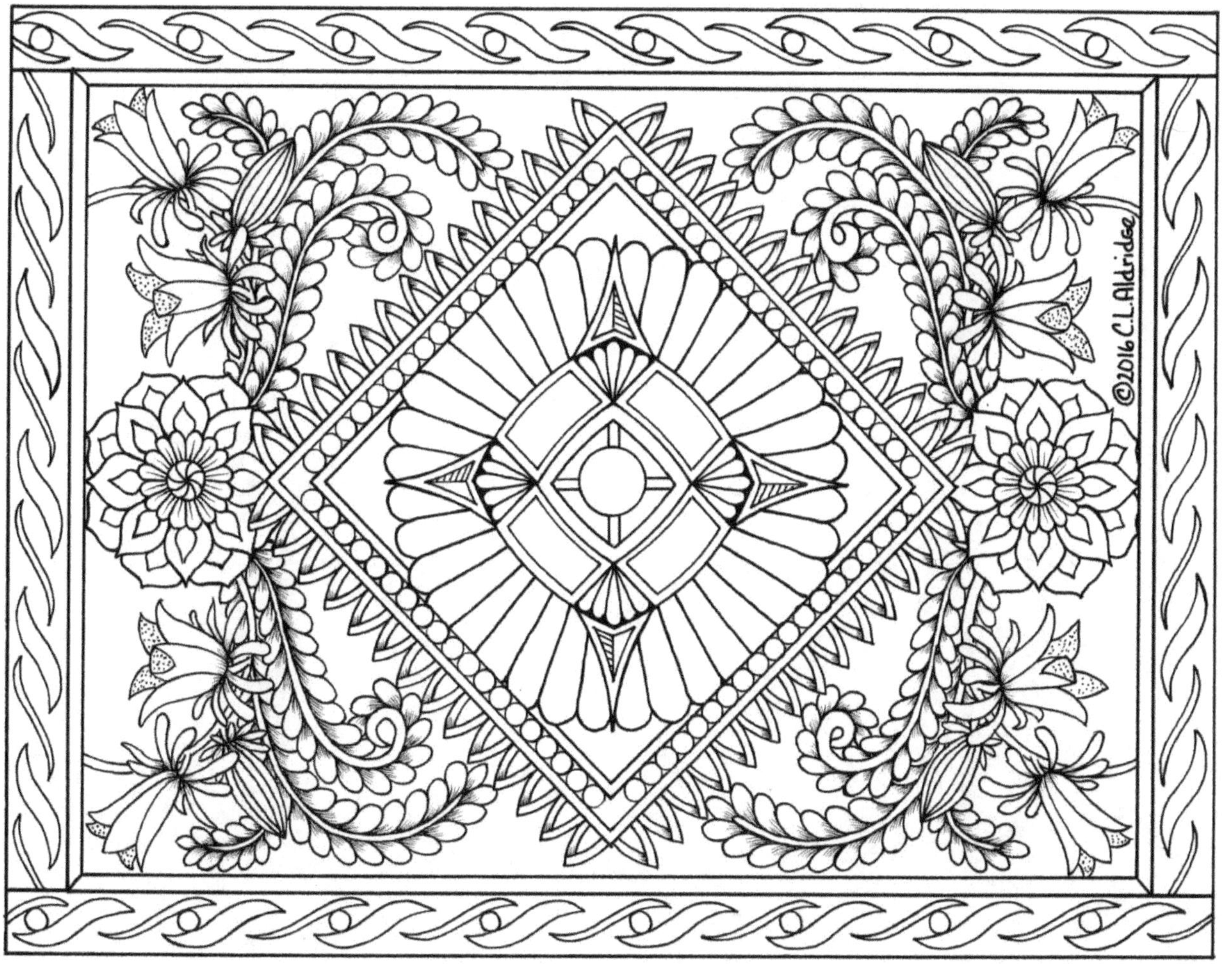

©2016 C.L. Aldridge

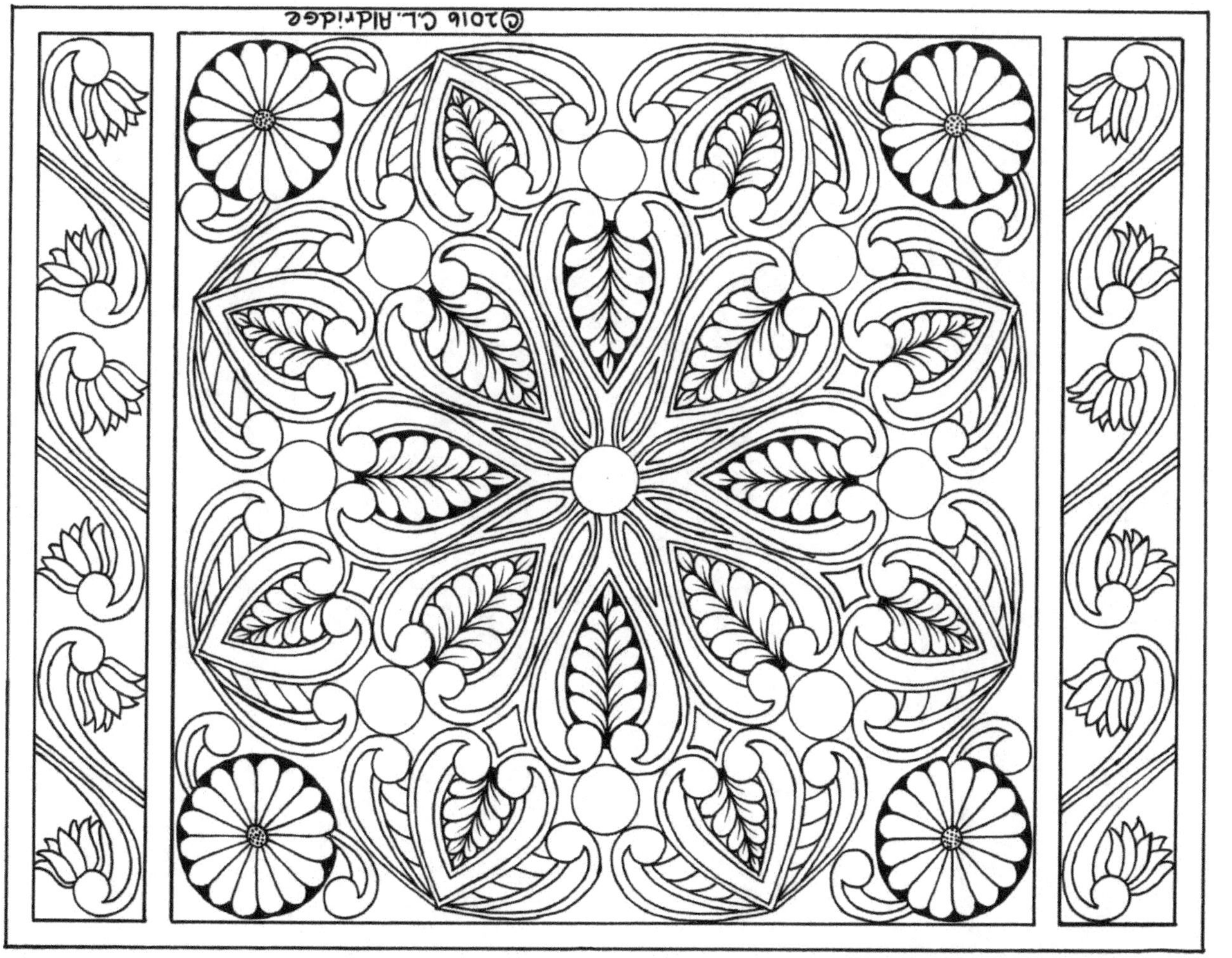

©2016 C.L. Aldridge

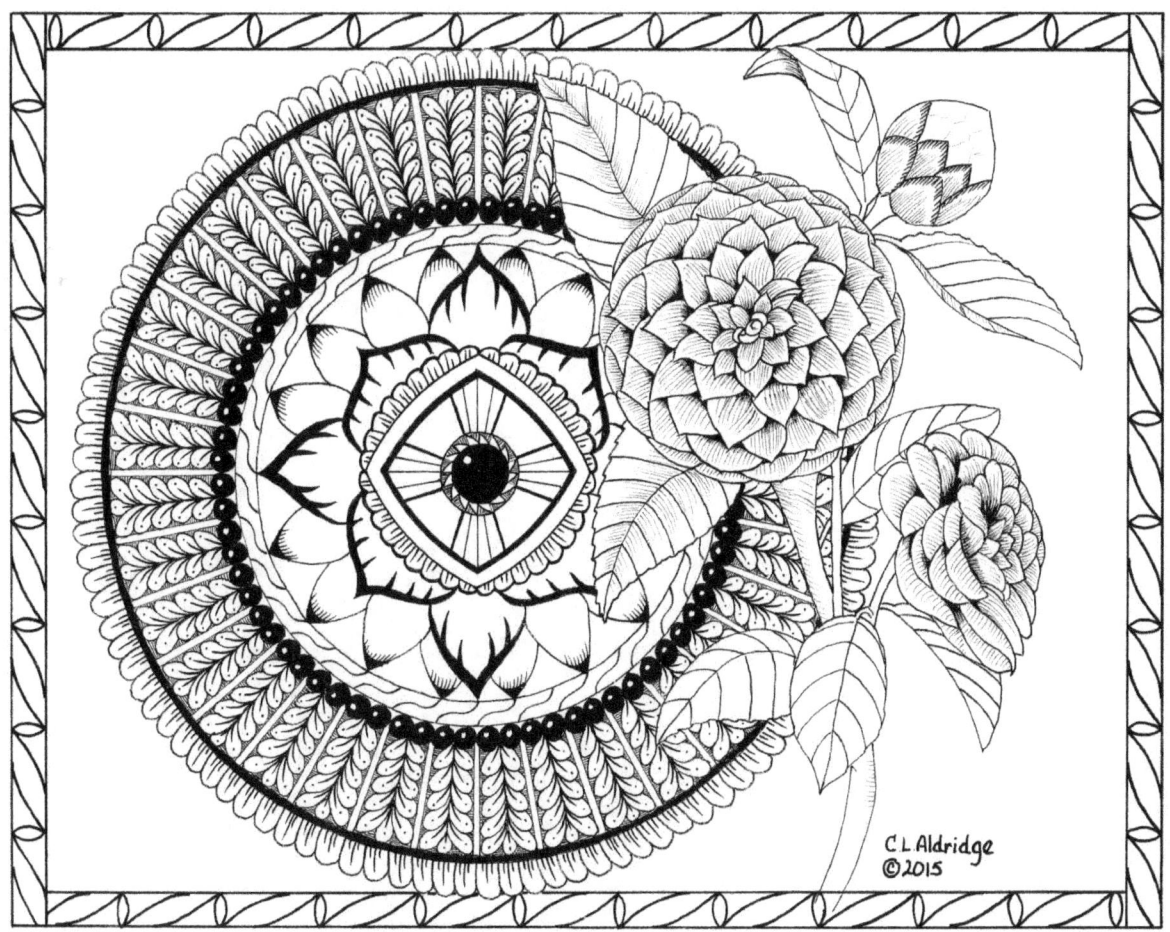

C L Aldridge
©2015

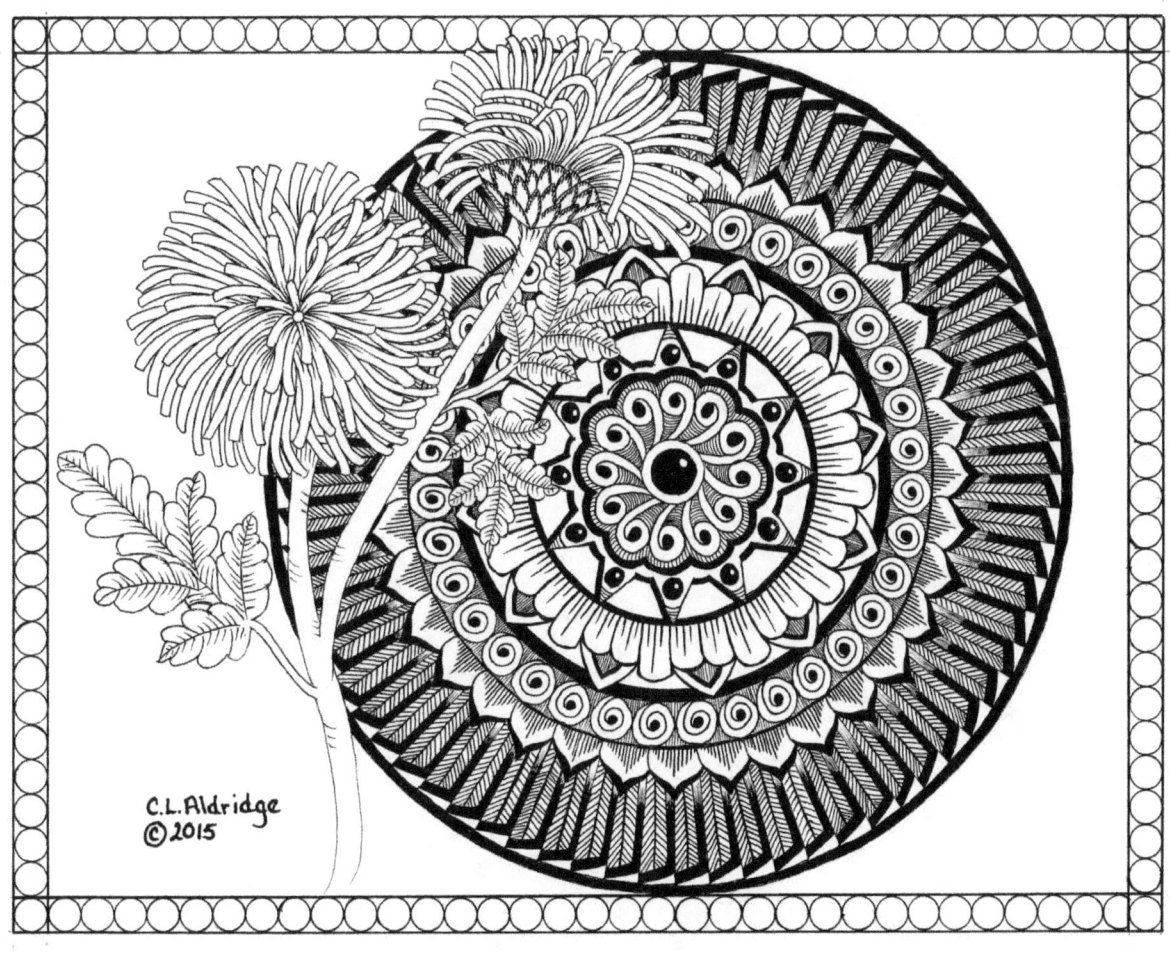

C.L. Aldridge
©2015

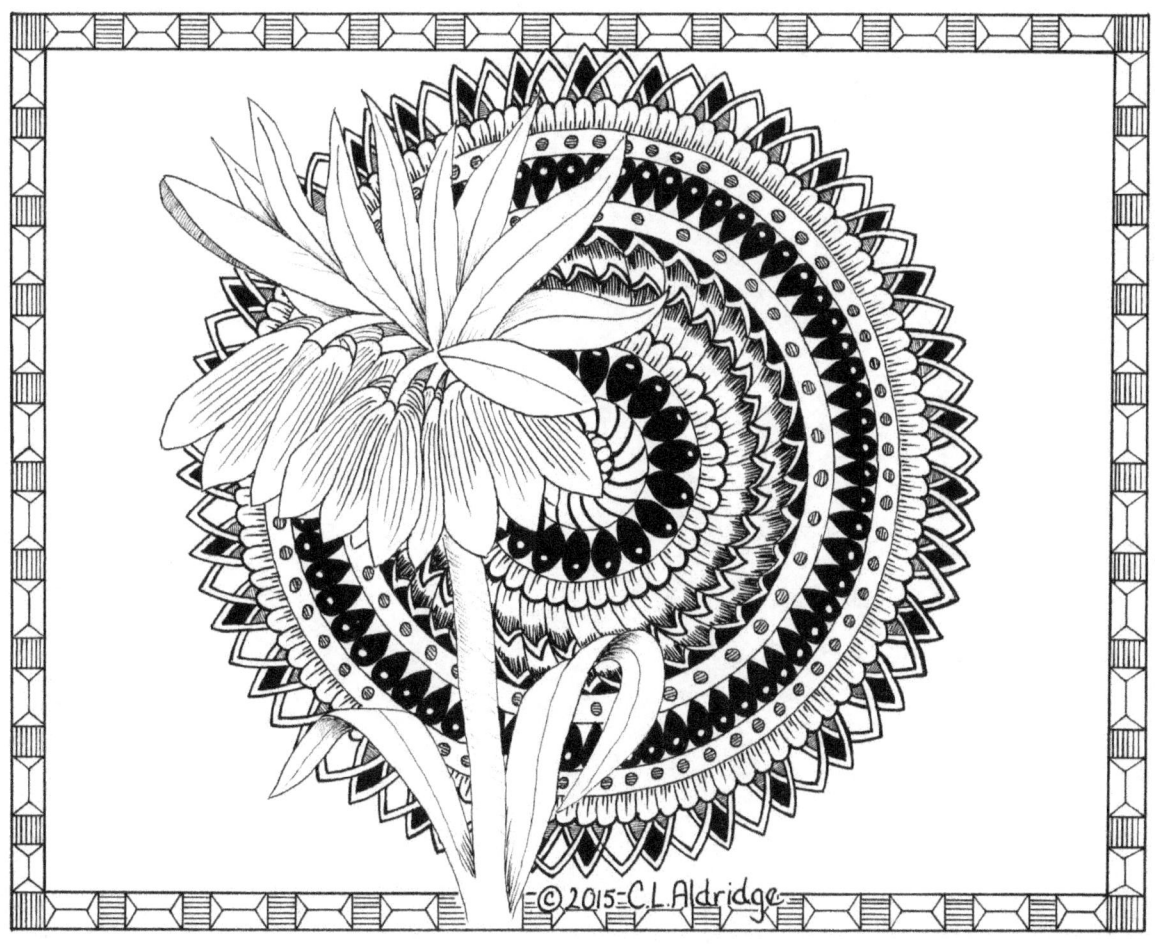

©2015 C.L.Aldridge

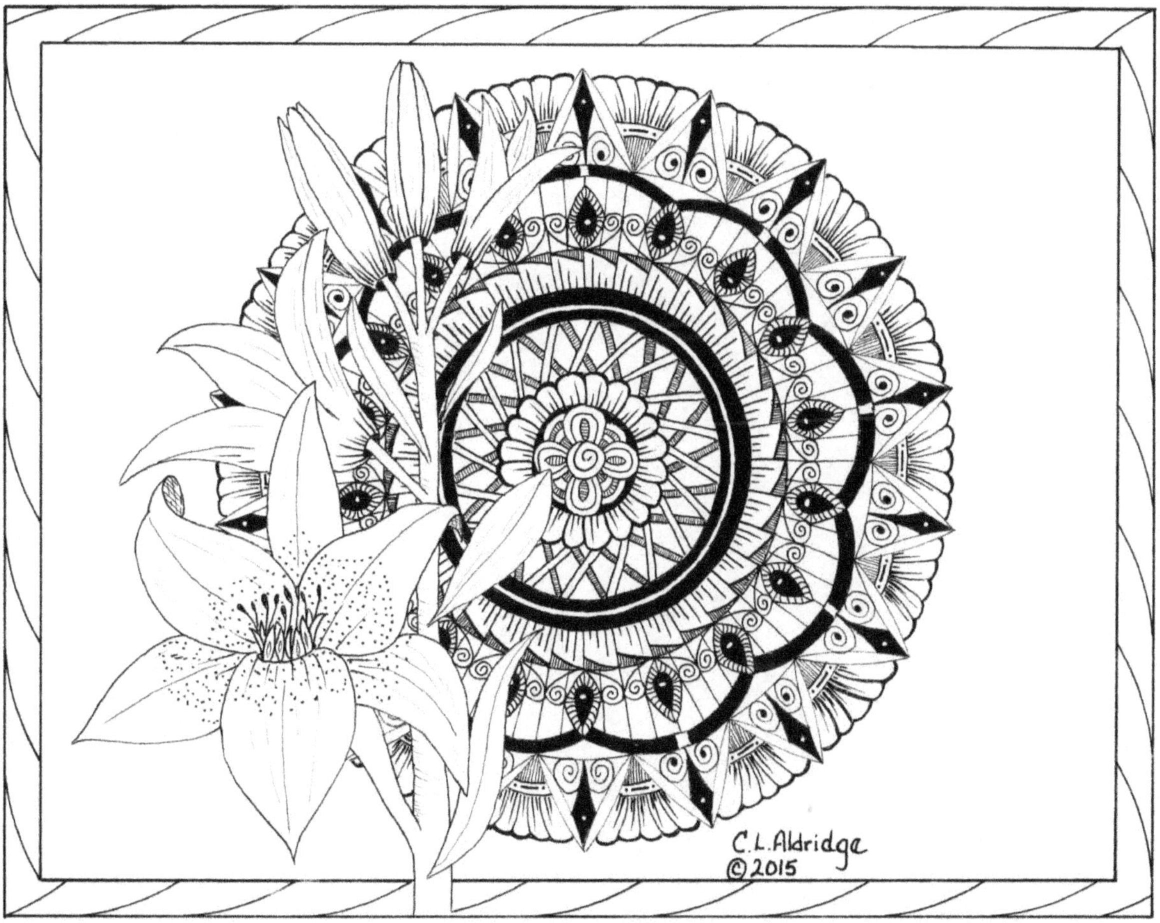

C.L.Aldridge
©2015

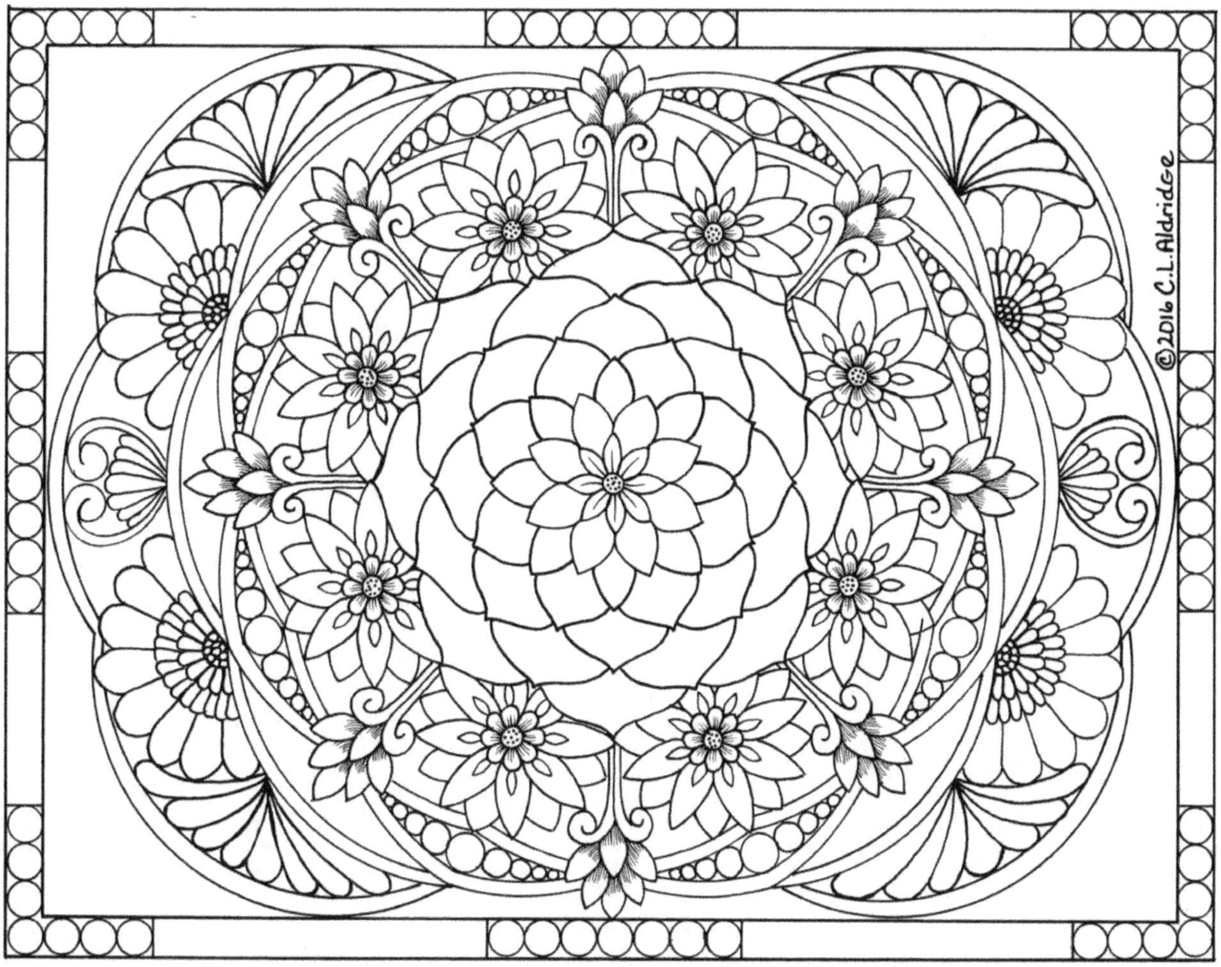
©2016 C.L.Aldridge

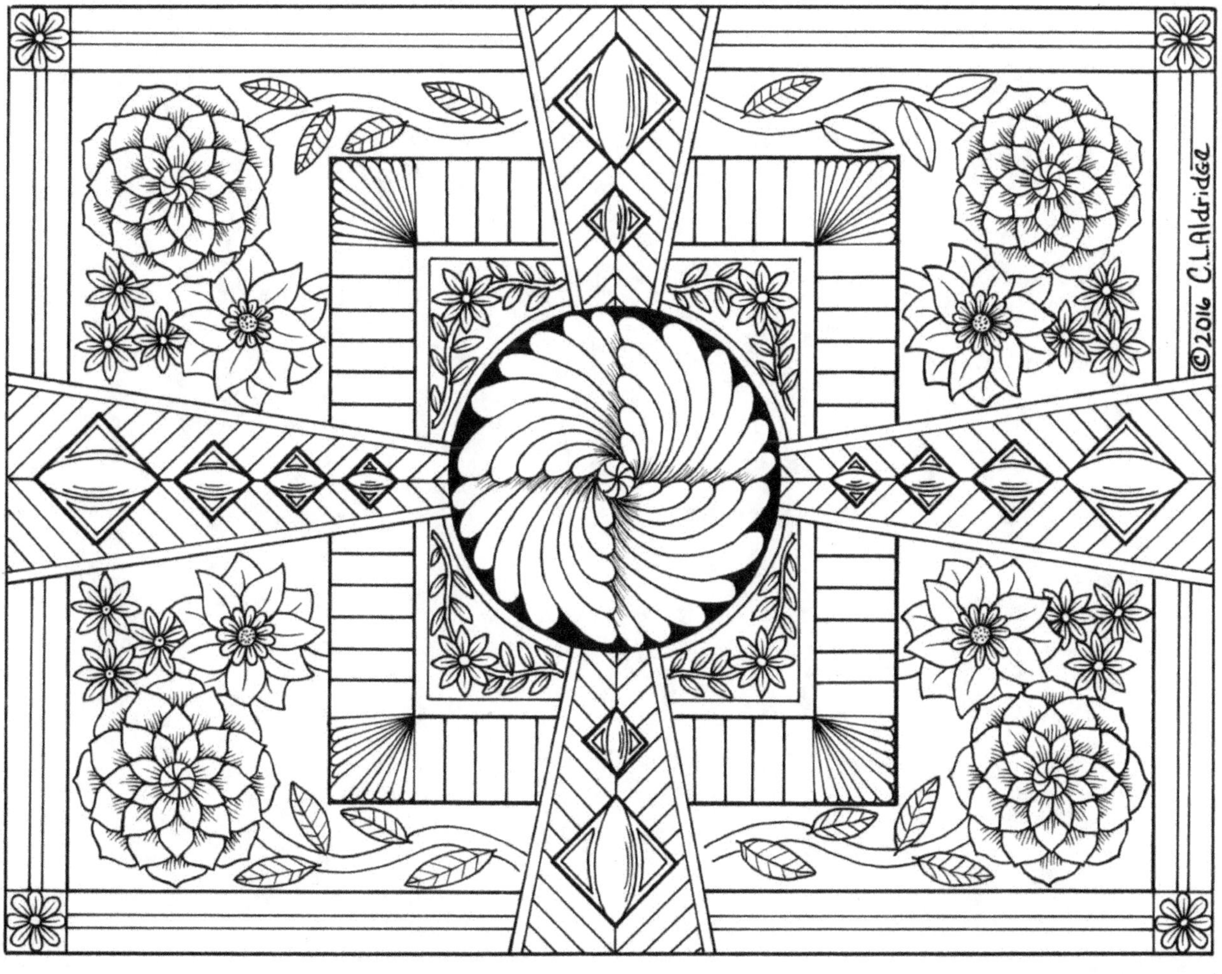
©2016 C.L.Aldridge

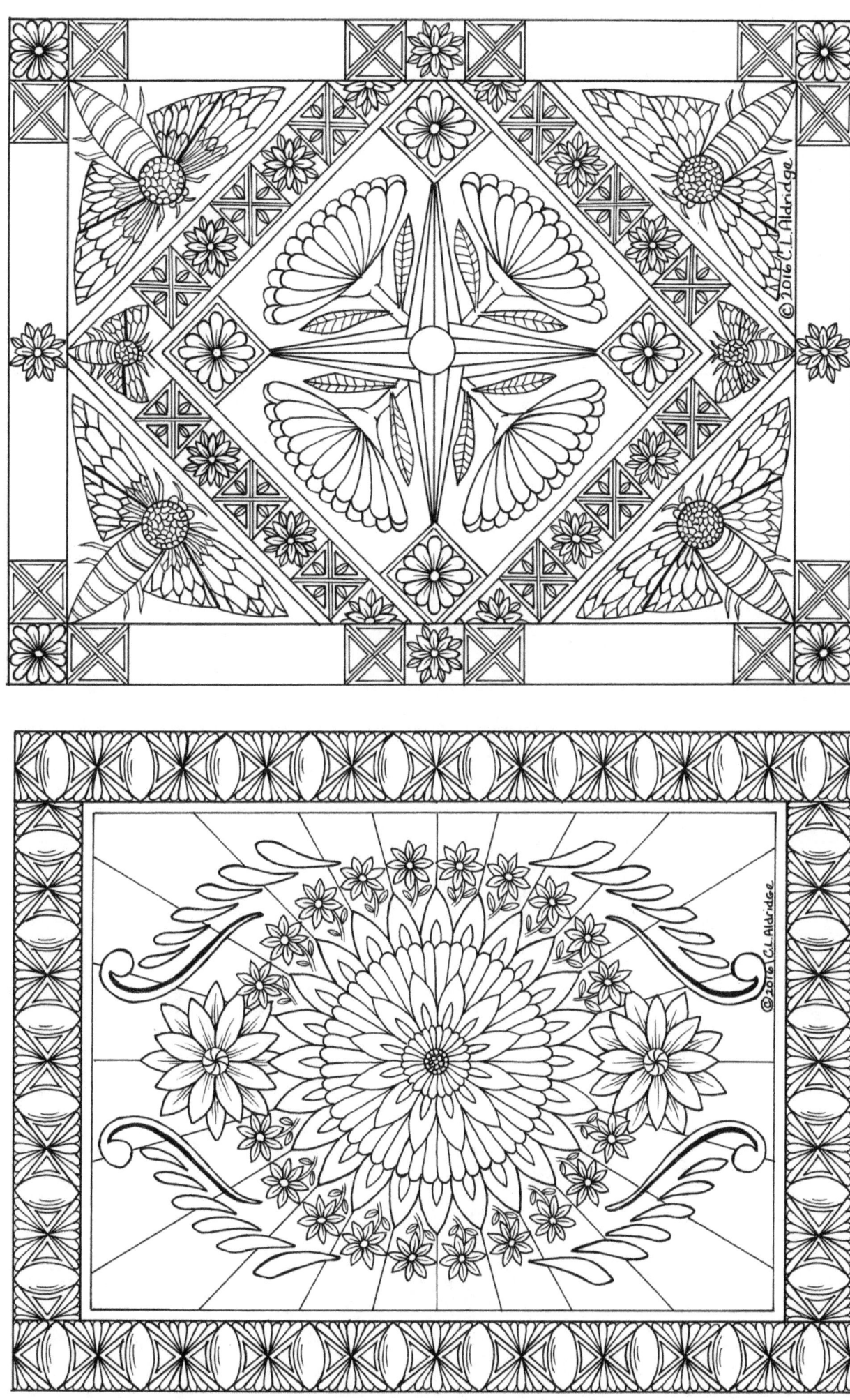

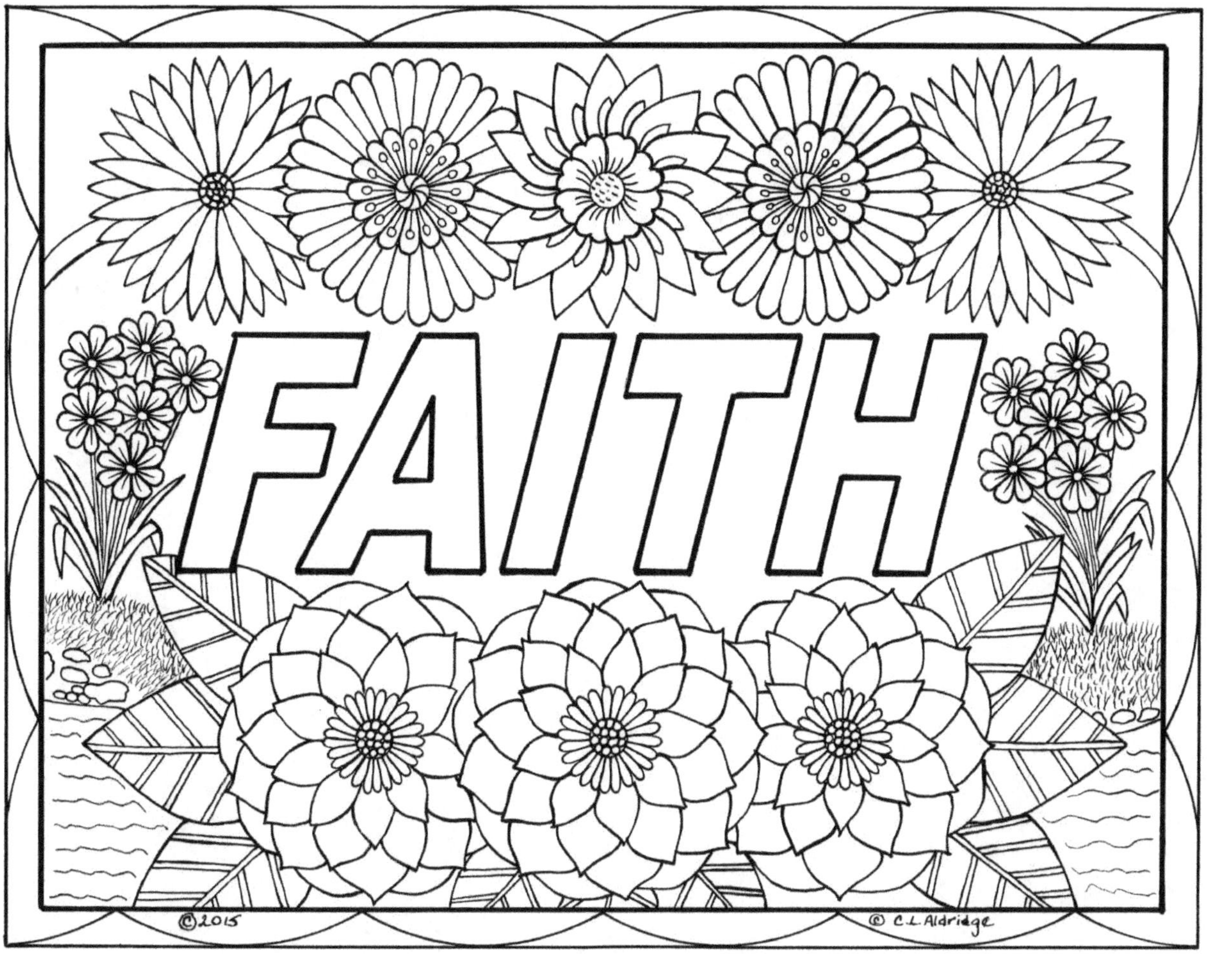

FAITH
©2015
© C.L. Aldridge

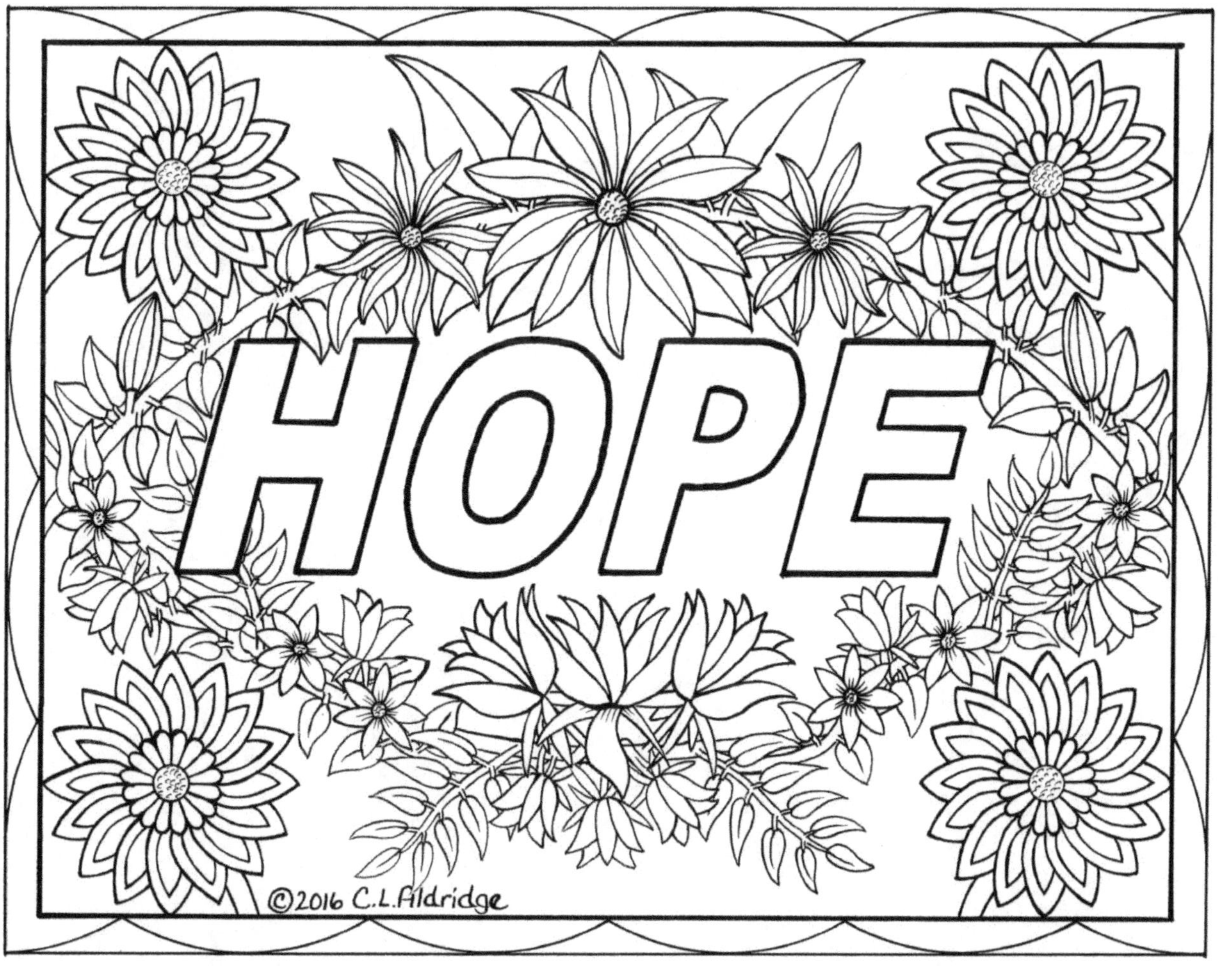

HOPE
©2016 C.L. Aldridge

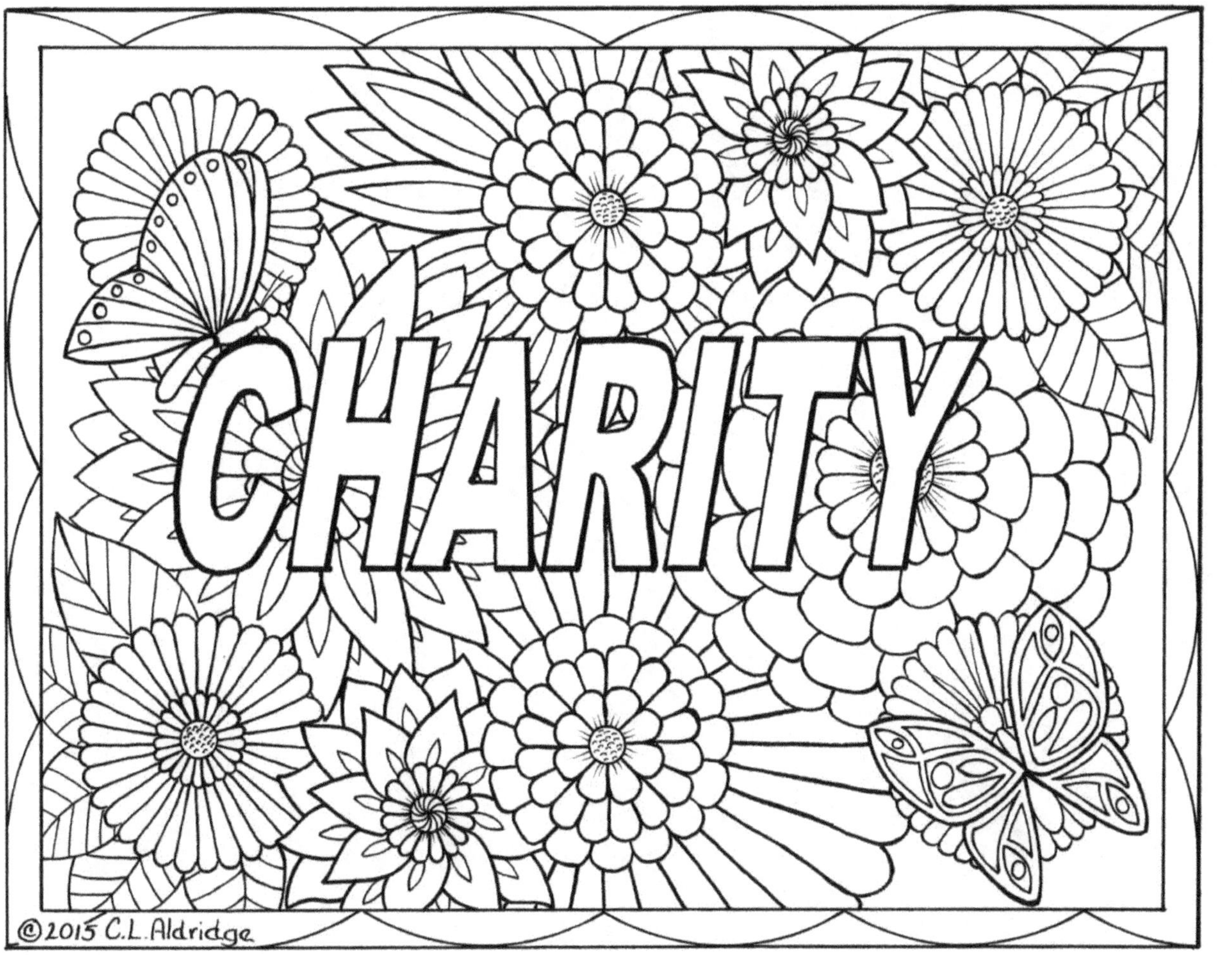

CHARITY

©2015 C.L.Aldridge

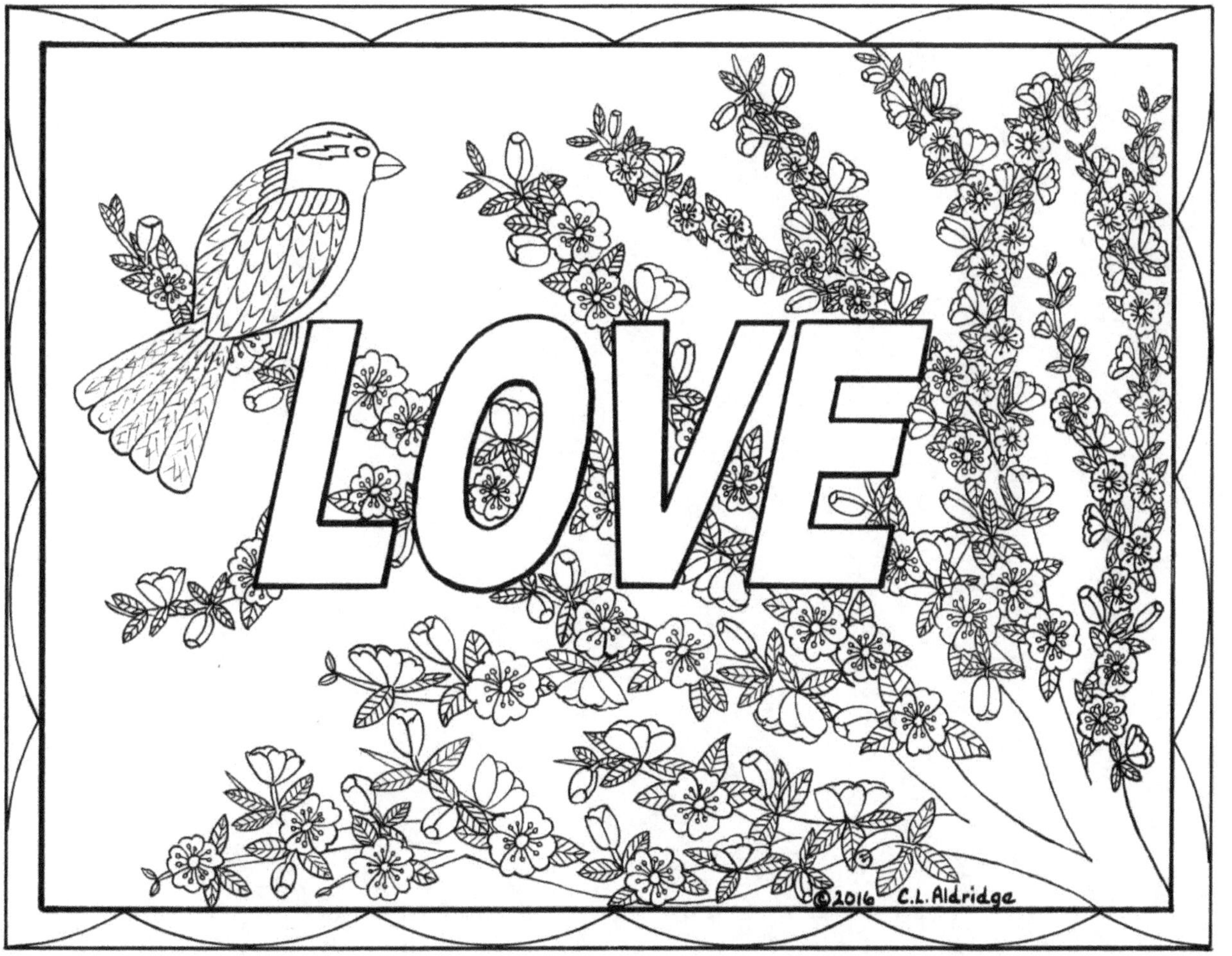

LOVE

©2016 C.L.Aldridge

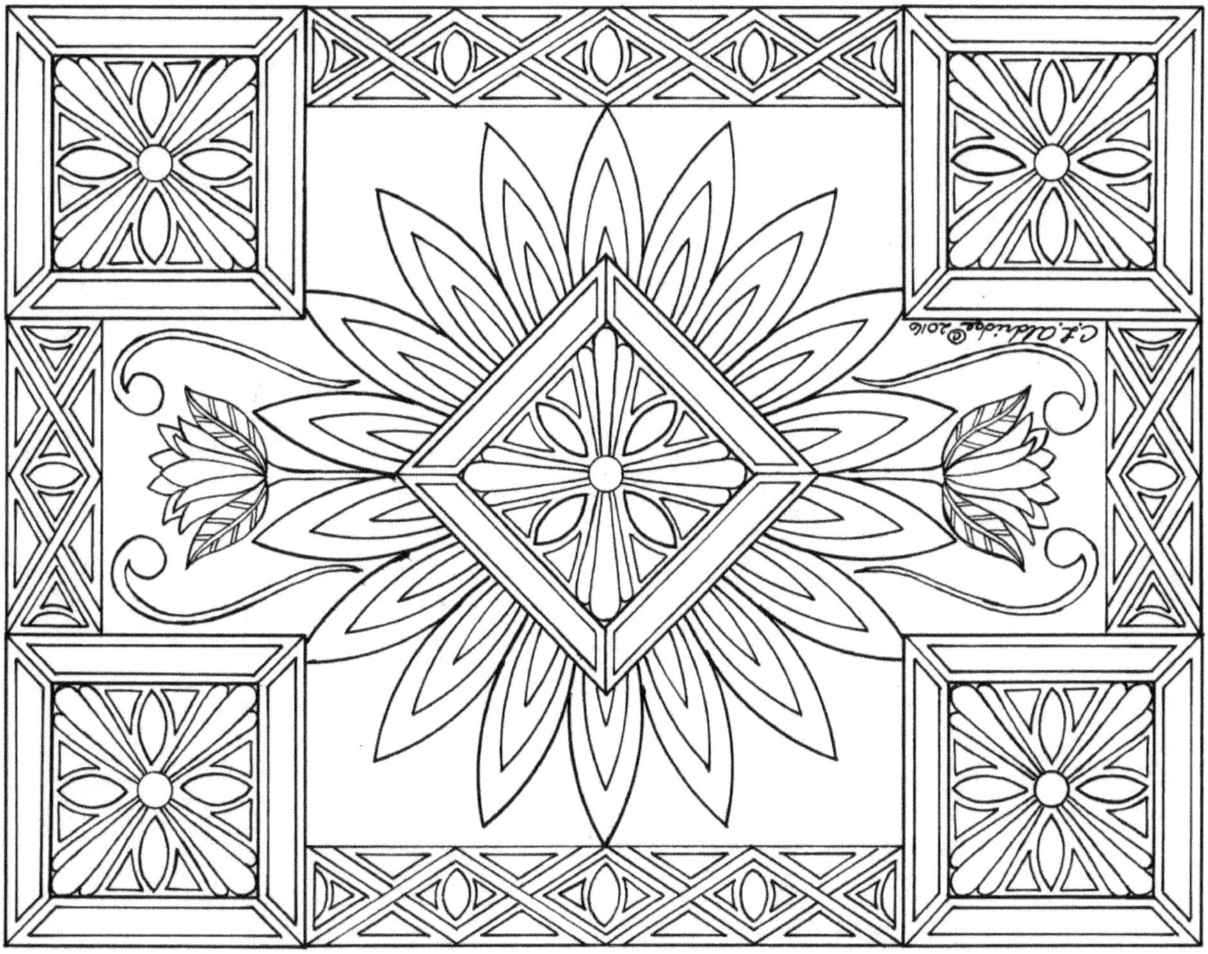

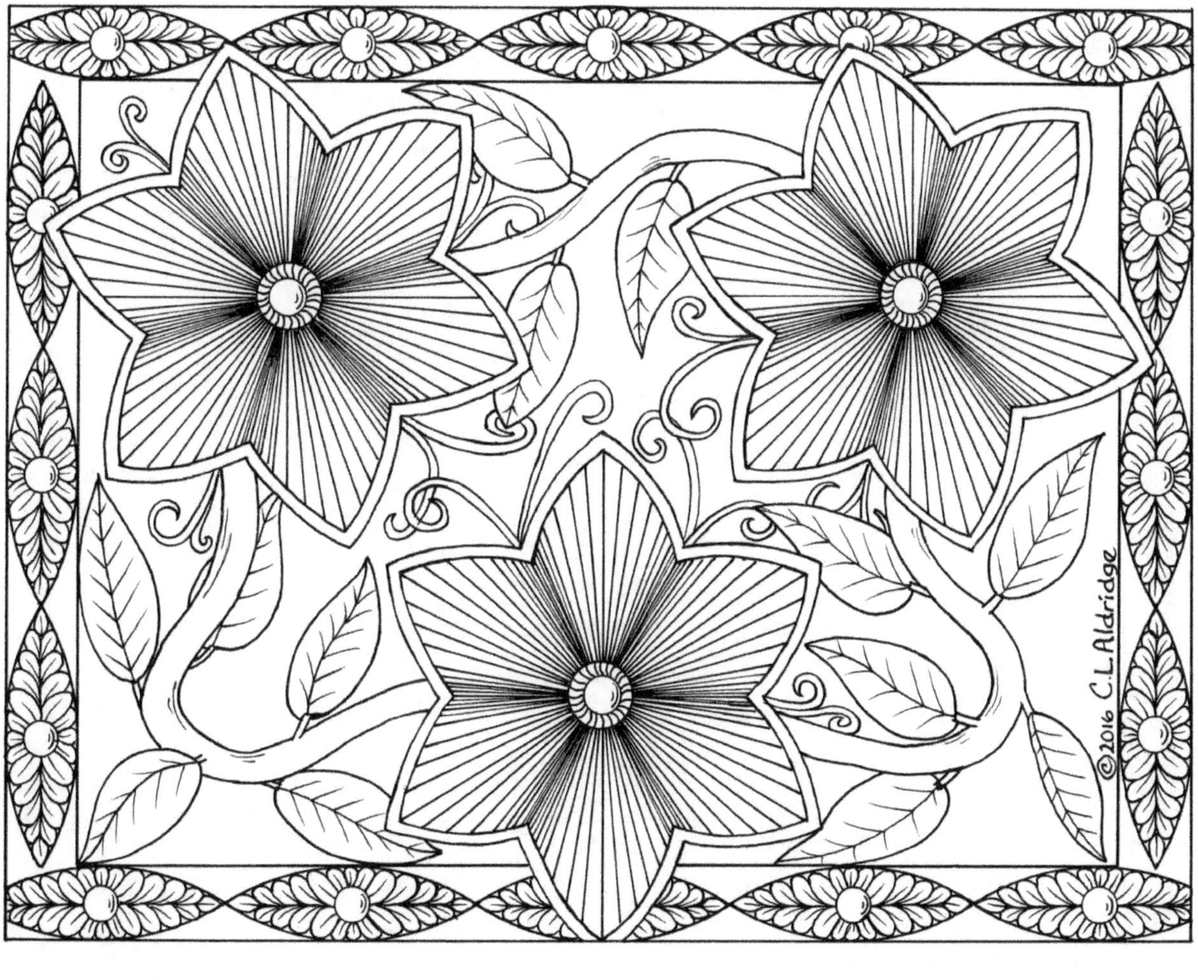

©2016 C.L.Aldridge

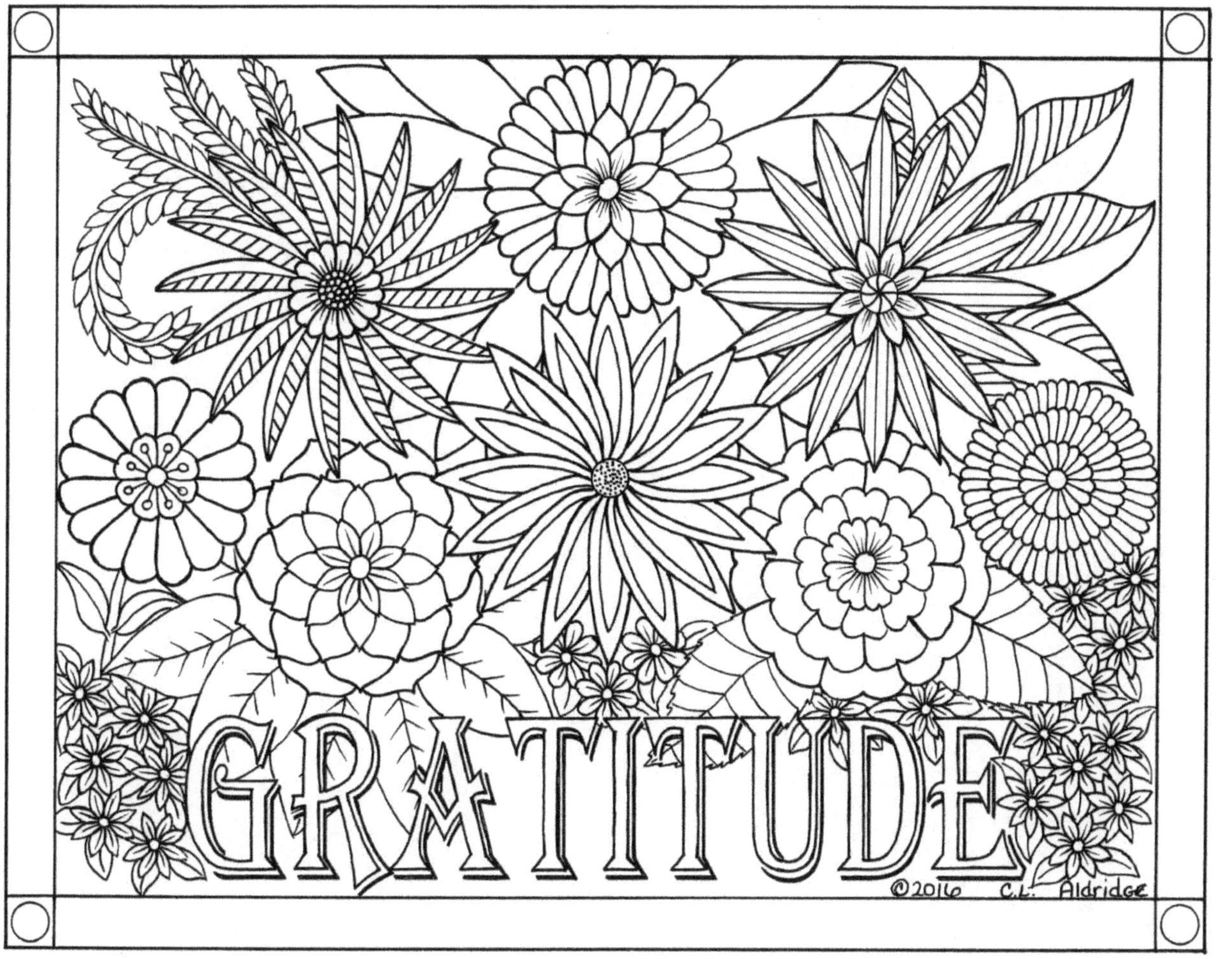

GRATITUDE

©2016   C.L. Aldridge

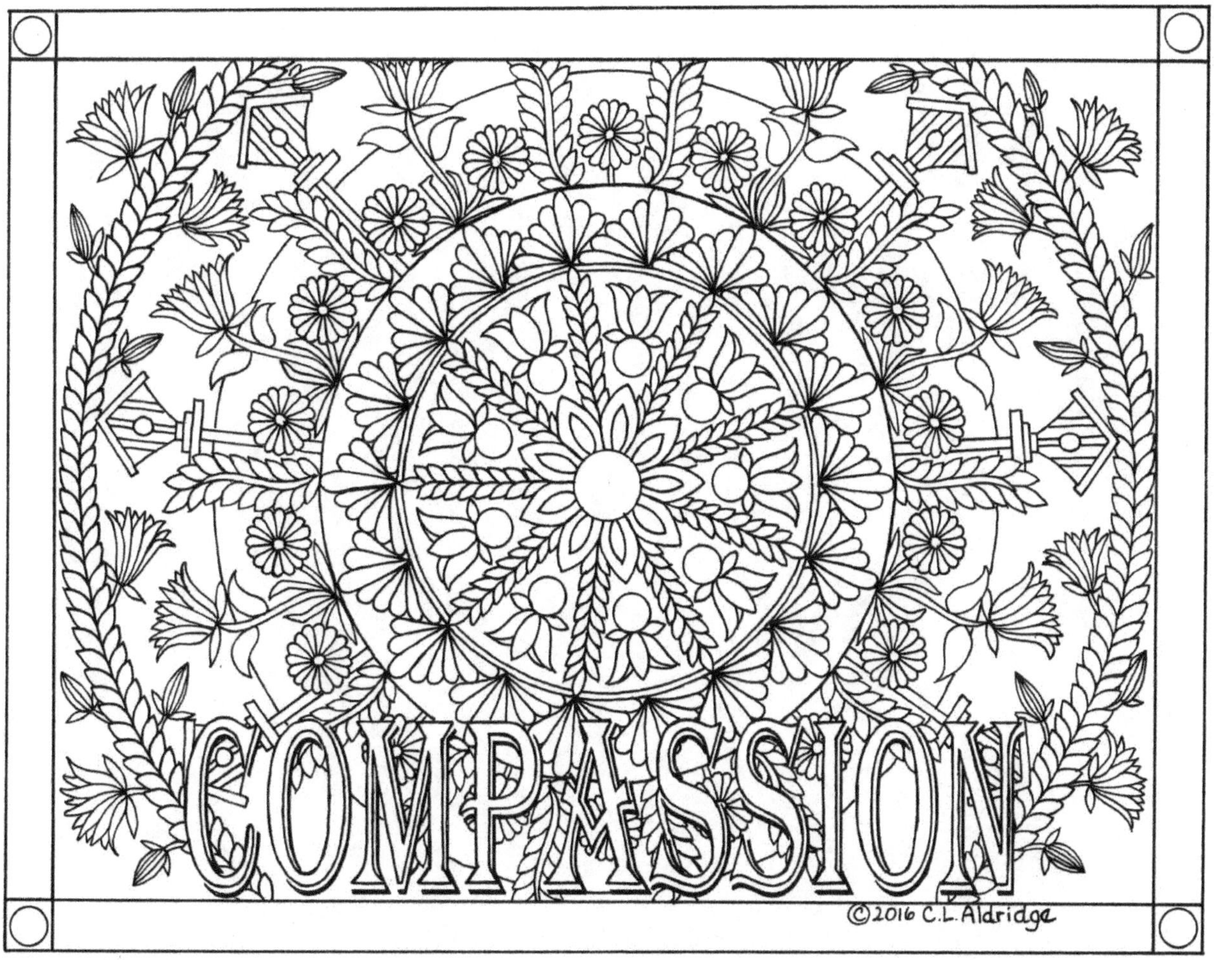

COMPASSION

©2016 C.L. Aldridge

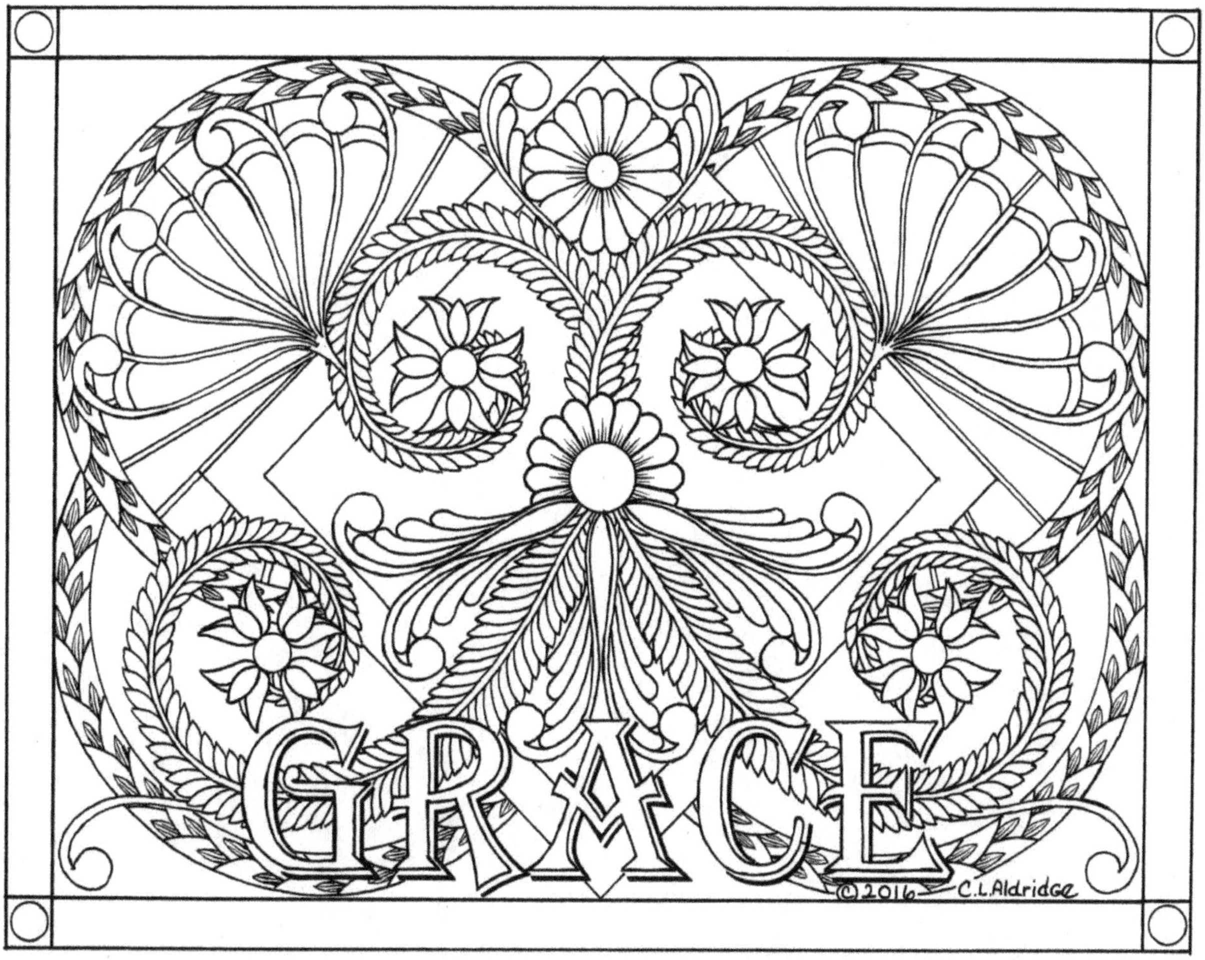

GRACE

©2016 C.L.Aldridge

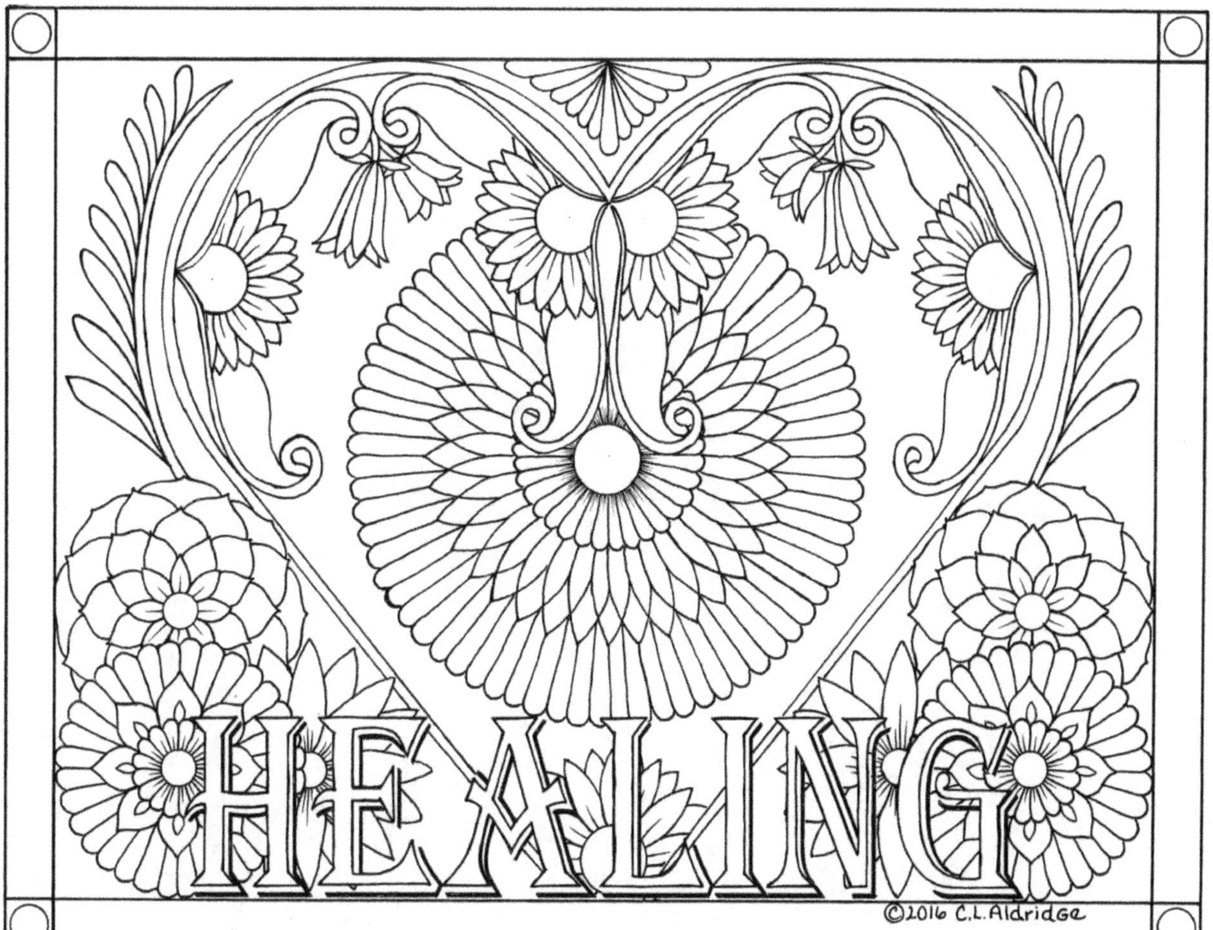

HEALING

©2016 C.L.Aldridge

This page has intentionally been left blank for use as either
a blotting page or color testing page.

This page has intentionally been left blank for use as either a blotting page or color testing page.

This page has intentionally been left blank for use as either
a blotting page or color testing page.

Don't miss my other Books

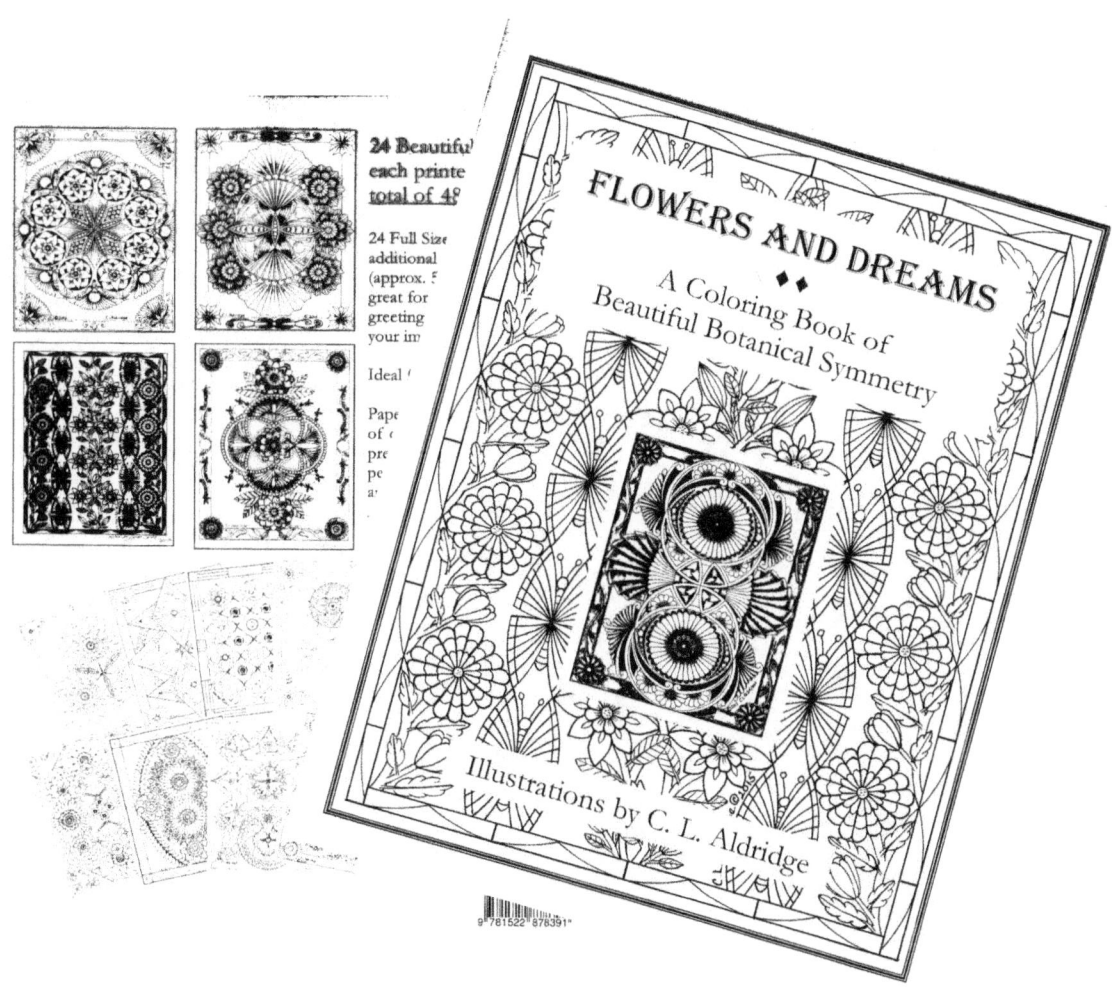

For more information, visit me
On the Web at: www.CLAldridgeArt.com
On Facebook at: www.Facebook.com/CLAldridgeArt
My Digital Site at: www.Etsy.com/Shop/CLAldridgeArt
Follow me on Instagram: @CLAldridgeArt

www.ingramcontent.com/pod-product-compliance
Lightning Source LLC
Chambersburg PA
CBHW080719190526
45169CB00006B/2432